Ad

Massachusetts Homebuyers Beware!
THE CARDS ARE STACKED AGAINST YOU

In this book, Tom takes the mystery out of many of the real estate industry's hidden secrets and educates homebuyers on exactly what they need to know to protect themselves and demand fair treatment when buying their next home.

—**Sam Schneiderman**
President/Principal Broker • Greater Boston Home Team

New house hunters need this book! Want to save money and avoid costly pitfalls? Tom Wemett opens his notebooks for you. He's been collecting ways for house hunters to save money as an Exclusive Buyer's Agent. You need to know what buyer's agents know and how you can benefit.

—**Rona Fischman**
Broker/Owner • 4 Buyers Real Estate, LLC

It has been said and written so often that it has become a cliché; however, it is true that for most consumers, buying a home is their biggest financial transaction. In *Massachusetts Homebuyers Beware!* Tom Wemett uses his forty-five years of real estate experience to educate Massachusetts homebuyers and reduce their financial risk by explaining twelve common homebuying errors.

—**Rich Rosa**
Co-founder • Buyers Brokers Only, LLC

I can't thank my friend and longtime colleague Tom Wemett enough for all his hard work producing the wonderful publication which is of such great benefit to consumers and those in our industry who are committed to providing client level service to buyers.

—**Bob Churchill**
Broker-Owner • Buyer Brokers of Cape Cod®, Churchill Associates, Inc.

continued on next page

I highly recommend all homebuyers read Tom's book, *Massachusetts Homebuyers Beware!* before they start the homebuying process. This book clearly lays out the steps you need to take in order to ensure you are informed, prepared, and protected as a buyer. There are many pitfalls for the unwary buyer, but if buyers follow Tom's wisdom as laid out in this book, they should be turning the key to their new home in no time!

—**Eric Asquith, Esq.**
Principal Broker • Monteleo Realty

Anyone with sufficient money can buy a home. That's not the problem. The problem is ending up with a home that meets your needs, for which you don't overpay, and that doesn't throw up nasty surprises after you move in. With care and expertise, *Massachusetts Homebuyers Beware!* by Tom Wemett guides you past these and all the common pitfalls buyers tumble into.

The fact is, every homebuyer's greatest need is for a trustworthy ally, someone who will provide advice and safe passage through the most costly investment most of us will ever make. Neither the listing agent nor the friendly selling agent can give you this — they are obligated to serve only the seller's best interests. Consequently, every day in every town and city, homebuyers make costly mistakes. For example, are you clear about which agent, if any, is on your side and which isn't? The answer surprises even "experienced" buyers.

Forget what some will tell you, homebuying is not a simple task! This book works for you! As a consumer advocate I give it my full endorsement.

—**Joseph Éamon Cummins**
Author of Not One Dollar More!
How to Save $3,000 to $30,000 Buying Your Next Home
purchase third edition at www.tomwemett.com/not-one-dollar-more

---

An important read for the new or experienced prospective homebuyer. Avoiding mistakes is another way of making the right decisions in an increasingly complex residential real estate environment.

—**Ken Riaf, Esq.**
Exclusive Buyer's Agent • Buyer's Choice Realty

The author, Tom Wemett, took a lot of time and effort in bringing these important topics to the forefront of what's needed in avoiding costly mistakes when buying a home.

—**Jerry M. Capone**
Mortgage Loan Officer • TD Bank

———————————

Anyone considering the purchase of real estate in Massachusetts should immediately buy a copy of *Massachusetts Homebuyers Beware!* Tom's true compassion for helping homebuyers is evident in this practical guide on the homebuying process that takes readers from developing a vision to a worry-free closing. The few hours spent to read this short book will reap huge rewards for homebuyers seeking a stress-free and informed avenue for buying real estate.

—**Kathleen Chiras**
CEO • Skyfor, Inc

———————————

Massachusetts Homebuyers Beware! is a very well written book for homebuyers. As one extremely well versed in real estate and mortgage loan origination, I found it a pleasure to see something written understandable to any reader. Topics truthfully covered will provide a good education for homebuyers looking for what to watch out for.

—**Clay Herbert**
Branch Manager • Academy Mortgage Corporation.

MASSACHUSETTS HOMEBUYERS BEWARE!

Richard,
To Your Success!
Tom W.

MASSACHUSETTS
HOMEBUYERS
BEWARE!
THE CARDS ARE STACKED AGAINST YOU

TOM WEMETT

Homebuyer Advisors LLC
Orange, Massachusetts

Homebuyer Advisors LLC
Post Office Box 72
Orange, MA 01364
info@tomwemett.com
www.tomwemett.com
978-633-9090

Cover design by NisseDesigns • www.nissedesigns.com
Edited and formatted by Haley's • haley.antique@verizon.net

ISBN, trade paper: 978-0-692-88828-5
ISBN, Kindle ebook: 978-0-9995831-0-4
Library of Congress Catalogue Number: pending

to Leo Berard

Contents

Leo Berard

Leo Berard, Pioneer in Representing Homebuyers

This book is dedicated to Leo Berard, a pioneer in providing real estate representation to homebuyers. Traditionally, real estate agents represented sellers and treated buyers as customers. In the mid 1980s, a few progressive real estate agents turned that around and began providing true representation of homebuyers. Leo was one of those dedicated individuals who felt that buyers deserved full representation as well.

Leo and his wife, Anne, founded Buyers Brokers of Cape Cod in the 1980s. He was a founding member and the first president of the Massachusetts Association of Buyer Agents (MABA) as well as subsequently a founding member and the first president of the National Association of Exclusive Buyer Agents (NAEBA).

Leo was an inspiration and mentor to dozens of real estate professionals who wanted to provide homebuyers with the highest legal, ethical, and moral representation. Leo was fond of saying, "We're on the side of the angels."

"Leo was an active mentor to most of the early exclusive buyer agents in Massachusetts. His generosity with his time and experience helped create the standard that exclusive buyer agents stand by to this day," according to one of his colleagues.

We all owe a debt of gratitude to Leo for his leadership, hospitality, kindness, and wisdom that encouraged many exclusive buyer agents to join the ranks of true homebuyer advocates.

We thank you, Leo, for leading the way.

Oh, what a tangled web we weave
when first we practice to deceive.

—Sir Walter Scott

Marmion

Who Can You Really Trust?

an introduction by Tom Wemett

Given the deeply ingrained sales culture of the traditional real estate industry, who can you really trust?

When a real estate *licensee* claims to be a buyer agent, is the *licensee* actually *your* agent or merely telling you something you want to hear in order to get your confidence and business?

Homebuyers I've worked for want to buy the right home at the right price. They don't want to find that, like the family on the cover of this book, they have been **SOLD** a home.

But when you look at traditional real estate industry ads, you see agents bragging about million dollar sales production, their latest hot listing for sale, and **SOLD** signs.

Then the same real estate *salespeople* turn around and tell you how one of them can be your buyer agent and save you lots of money. Really?

If you were selling a home, then such ads and the traditional real estate industry's deeply ingrained sales culture might appeal to you.

So be forewarned—*Massachusetts Homebuyers Beware! The cards are in fact stacked against you.*

My goal in writing this book is to reshuffle the cards, help flip the odds back in your favor, provide you with information that will help you buy the right home at the right price, and provide you with knowledge so you can find the right agent who will help you do just that.

After more than forty-five years as a licensed real estate broker in three different states and the past twenty-five years representing homebuyers only, I have identified the dozen mistakes most often made by homebuyers.

I'll describe the areas of concern and provide you with information you need to avoid mistakes other homebuyers have made so that you obtain the best outcome to your homebuying adventure.

One of the areas I'll spend considerable time on (in *Chapter Five • Find and Work with a True Loyal Agent™*) is describing a type of real estate agent that you are probably not aware of.

I coined the name *True Loyal Agent™* to distinguish such agents from traditional real estate industry *licensee-salespersons*.

The right agent is one who legally must be loyal to you and be your protector at all times and in every situation. Such an agent has chosen to provide a higher level of duties and service than the traditional real estate *licensee* can provide or wants to provide.

Such agents constitute less than one percent of all real estate *licensees*. If you want the best outcome to your homebuying adventure, you must understand who they are, why it is important to work with them, and how to find and make sure you are working with one of them.

As you continue to read this book, you will find references to online sources underlined and noted in blue. They are summarized at the end of the book in a chapter entitled

Online Resources for Massachusetts Homebuyers Beware. They are also available as hot, clickable links to the referenced websites online at www.tomwemett.com/online-resources.

It is possible that links to some online resources noted in this book do not work because they have changed. At press time, the links worked. To account for the possibility that published links do not work, I will keep links current and updated at the website noted above.

So let's get started. You may have already made the decision to buy a home, but it still makes sense to start with *Chapter One • Develop a Clear Homebuying Vision* to make sure you achieve your goal to buy the best home at the best possible price and that your homebuying adventure is exciting, satisfying, enjoyable, and successful.

Chapter One
Develop a Clear Homebuying Vision

If you are like some homebuyers, you may go about buying a home without giving it much thought beforehand. Perhaps your parents own a home and your friends and co-workers are buying homes, so perhaps you should, too, may characterize your thinking.

However, it takes a clearer vision to make solid plans for a home purchase. Perhaps waiting one or two years or more makes sense.

When I talk about vision, I'm not really talking about details about the home you might like, as that comes later.

I believe that vision starts with deciding *why* you want to buy a home in the first place.

Buying a home shouldn't be taken lightly. Buying a home, whether it is your first or even if you have owned a home previously, will probably be the largest purchase you will ever make. It just makes sense to think very carefully about such a purchase before deciding to go ahead.

Buying a home should not be an impulse purchase or based on emotion; rather, a home purchase should be a deliberate, well-thought-out decision with a specific plan of action that includes a reasonable time frame.

You need time to research the process, to get into the best position to buy, and then to take the right steps to ensure the best outcome, which is buying the right home at the right price on the best terms. You don't want to be sold a home or pushed into buying before being prepared.

The first step is to decide if you want to be a homeowner. There are advantages to renting over owning that anyone should consider before deciding to take on the responsibility of owning.

Advantages of Renting

- You don't have yard work or repair issues as a renter unless you are responsible for them in your lease.

  Your landlord is generally responsible for all maintenance and repair costs, including such things as appliances, heating and air conditioning, plumbing and electrical, roof repairs, and more.

- You don't pay homeowner's insurance or liability or flood insurance when you rent.

  Instead, you may have renter's insurance to cover personal liability and your personal items.

  Renter's insurance costs much less than homeowner's insurance.

- As a renter, you don't directly pay real estate taxes, although it could be argued that you do via the rent payment you make.

  But it is without the benefit of being able to deduct the cost of real estate taxes when you file your income tax.

- When you rent, you don't have the risk of a downturn in the real estate market causing you to end up with a home worth less than the mortgage you owe on it.

- You aren't tied down to one location when you rent.

  At the end of your lease, you are free to move.

  If you own a home and need or want to move, it is a far more complicated process, because you have to decide what to do with the house you own.

- You may not be able to afford a home if you want to live in an urban area where the cost of buying a home could be prohibitive.

  Renting may be your best and perhaps only option.

- You may have access to amenities such as a pool, tennis courts or fitness center when you rent that you otherwise wouldn't have as a home owner.

  Such amenities could cost you thousands of dollars more as a home owner instead of a renter in a complex when such amenities are supplied as part of the rent or at a very low additional cost.

- You don't need as much money up front to rent rather than buy a home. Even with a loan requiring a low or no down payment, you need cash for closing costs, real estate tax and insurance escrows, and moving expenses.

  When renting, you need the cost of the security deposit, (usually one month) along with moving expenses, and you can move in.

Then there are the arguments in favor of buying a home. David Bach, the author of the best-selling book *The Automatic Millionaire Homeowner*, a book I highly recommend, believes very strongly that buying a home is an investment that everyone can benefit from.

He thinks that not prioritizing homeownership is "the single biggest mistake millennials are making." Bach warns: "If millennials don't buy a home, their chances of actually having any wealth in this country are little to none."

As he writes in *The Automatic Millionaire*, "As a renter, you can easily spend half a million dollars or more on rent over the years ($1,500 a month for 30 years comes to $540,000) and in the end wind up just where you started—owning nothing. Or you can buy a house and spend the same amount paying down a mortgage and in the end wind up owning your own home free and clear!"

The Federal Reserve's September 2014 Survey of Consumer Finances found that the median net worth of renters was $5,400 while the median net worth of homeowners was $195,400.

Advantages of Homeownership

- Tax Advantages – your mortgage interest and real estate taxes are deductible on your income tax return at the time of this writing.

  However, the tax deduction may or may not be advantageous for you depending on your income tax situation. If you don't itemize but simply take the standard deduction, then the only increase in tax advantages will be based on the actual increase in deductible expenses that the mortgage interest and real estate taxes comprise over the standard deduction you already take.

But if you already itemize deductions then you will be able to reap additional tax advantages from the increase in deductible expenses that mortgage interest and real estate taxes add to current itemized deductions.

Talk to a professional tax adviser to review your financial situation to see to what advantage, if any, owning a home might make in your annual tax situation.

- Forced Savings – Just as you pay your rent on time to avoid being evicted from your apartment, you will do whatever it takes to pay your mortgage on time as well to avoid being foreclosed on and losing your home.

The difference of course is that you will be building equity in your home each month as you make your monthly mortgage payments.

Part of each payment is a principal payment reducing the amount that you owe and increasing the equity in the home (the difference between the value of your home and the balance owed on the mortgage).

- Building Asset Value – Besides having part of each mortgage payment reducing what you owe on the mortgage and thus increasing your equity, there are two more ways that may increase your equity.

The first is "forced appreciation" by means of improvements you make to the home. You force the increase in value and equity you have in the home by means of improving the property and its value. The actual value added by means of your direct labor is often referred to as "sweat equity."

Whether you pay someone else or do the work yourself, improvements that actually upgrade the property and aren't limited to conditions that only satisfy your specific tastes and needs should result in an increase in value.

The second is "market appreciation," which occurs when the overall market for real estate is increasing and, thus, the value of your home increases as well.

The real estate market goes in cycles, up and down. We recently saw the market drop drastically in 2007 and 2008. But in most real estate markets across the country, prices have rebounded, and in some urban areas buyers are paying prices that exceed asking prices by ten or twenty percent or more.

- Pride of Ownership – Although most people take pride in their home whether renting or owning, there are advantages to owning.

Any repairs or improvements you make to the apartment may benefit you temporarily while you live there, but overall they benefit the landlord more than they do you, provided the improvements really are improvements that the landlord doesn't have to redo.

By owning a home, you in essence become your own landlord, and any repairs, replacements or improvements directly benefit you.

By owning rather than renting, you have the ability to plant a garden, paint whatever colors you want, make whatever improvements you want, have whatever pets you want, and do whatever you want with your property subject, of course, to local zoning and building codes and regulations.

Buying Now or Waiting

So what is *your* vision of owning your own home? What is your reason if your decision is to buy a home? Have you seriously taken into consideration renting vs owning? Are you making a deliberate rather than emotional decision to buy a home? Are you willing to be patient if things don't quite work out ideally for you right now? If so, then you should be ready to take the next steps to get you closer to actually buying your own home.

But before you continue, you really do need to assess whether waiting would put you into a more advantageous position.

- Are you in a financial position to buy a home today, or do you need to wait a while?

- Perhaps you don't have enough money saved to be comfortable taking on the financial responsibility of buying a home.

- If your employment is questionable, you may want to wait a while to make sure your income source is stable.

- Are you considering a new job? It would be best to wait until you are in the new job for a while to make sure you are comfortable in your new surroundings.

    If you are changing careers, it may be difficult to get a mortgage unless you have a track record in your line of work.

    A potential lender may want to wait to see how your work situation develops.

- Are you due a raise in pay or a bonus such that waiting a while might make buying a home less financially stressful?

- Are you due a large income tax refund that you want to use to buy a home with?

- Do you have credit issues that may need time and effort to correct and improve?

- Are you in a lease that doesn't expire for another year with no provision to leave early or cancel the lease without it costing you a lot of money or forfeiting your security deposit?

If the answer is yes to any of the above questions, you may want to delay your home purchase.

That's okay.

Remember that buying a home is the most expensive purchase you will probably ever make.

The decision to buy a home should be deliberate.

But don't just sit and wait.

Take steps discussed here to get yourself ready to buy when one or more of the above timing issues has been resolved.

Chapter Two

Check and Improve Your Credit Scores

Homebuyers often wait until they have a property under contract or until they apply for a mortgage to check their credit reports.

If errors or problems arise, great delays and heartaches can result.

It can take upwards of five months to get inaccurate information removed from credit reports and even longer for credit scores to readjust and increase to sufficient worthiness to qualify for a mortgage or reduced interest rate.

In the meantime, the seller probably won't wait and you may have already spent money on inspections.

And you still haven't bought a home.

You should obtain a copy of credit reports and credit scores early in the process.

Generally, credit score means the FICO score, a number based on a formula developed by the Fair Isaac Corporation, an analytics software company that provides industry-acknowledged summaries of credit accounts and payment history.

The FICO credit score determines access to and cost of credit.

A higher credit score often means paying a lower interest rate.

Most lenders use the FICO credit score as the main basis for loan or credit approvals, so the higher the FICO score, the better, and the lower, the more problems.

FICO scores range from 300-850, and Fair Isaac calculates them for each of the three big credit-reporting agencies: TransUnion, Equifax, and Experian.

Lenders generally take the three scores and use the middle score to evaluate credit worthiness.

Lenders often work from a grid showing credit score ranges and down payment percentages to determine the interest rate for a loan or the amount of points you need to pay to get a better interest rate.

For more information about credit reporting and credit scores go to: www.myfico.com/credit-education/credit-report-credit-score-articles/.

Determining a FICO Score

- Thirty-five percent determined by payment history—Do you regularly pay bills on time to any creditor that submits information to the credit bureau? Overdue medical bills, utility bills, and other bills may diminish the payment history component of a credit score.

- Thirty percent based on the amounts owed each of your creditors in comparison with the total credit line of each creditor—if you're maxing out credit cards, your score may suffer.

It appears that the ideal is keep balances below thirty percent of the maximum credit line.

- Fifteen percent determined by the length of credit history, both the age of each account and how recent any activity—the fewer and older the accounts, the better.

- Ten percent based on how many recently opened accounts compared with the total number of accounts as well as the number of recent inquiries made by lenders—your score can drop if it looks as if you're seeking several new sources of credit, a sign that you may be in financial trouble.

  If a lender initiates an inquiry about your credit report without your knowledge, though, it should not affect your score, as with credit offers.

  Shopping around for a mortgage shouldn't hurt, either, if you keep your search within a six-week period or less.

  Each inquiry for a credit card however can negatively impact the score, so be selective.

- Ten percent involving the types of credit used—having installment debt like a mortgage with a fixed amount each month demonstrates ability to manage a large loan.

  How a debtor handles revolving debt, like credit cards, tends to carry weight as more predictive of future behavior. Do you pay off the balance each month or the minimum, for example? Do you charge to the limit of cards or rarely use them?

Other Considerations

- You shouldn't take on new credit or apply for credit in the months leading to the decision to buy a home and especially during the time you have a home under contract.

  I've had buyers buy a new car while their mortgage application was under process.

  The new loan came to the attention of the mortgage company, and the buyers didn't qualify for the mortgage due to higher debt-to-income ratios, explained in *Chapter Three • Understand Your Financing Options.*

  Because they didn't qualify for sufficient credit and had no other resources to purchase the home, the prospective buyers lost the home.

  Buyers may also end up losing a deposit if they are no longer qualified for a loan and the period of loan contingency expired.

  Mortgage companies routinely request a credit report just before closing a loan in case the prospective buyers have taken out new loans since the original credit report.

- You shouldn't deposit large amounts of cash in a bank account near closing.

Major cash deposits require a paper trail. I discuss the topic in more detail in *Chapter Three • Understanding Your Financing Options.*

• You shouldn't co-sign loans for anyone. Payments made on those loans, even though made by someone else, will count against your debt-to-income ratios and could cause problems with approval for a mortgage.

• You shouldn't change banks during or just before applying for a mortgage. If the lender requires an account at the lending institution in order to obtain a loan or better interest rate, keep the existing account open until after the loan closes.

• You shouldn't close credit accounts. Closing accounts could negatively impact credit scores especially if they are older accounts.

Part of the credit score calculation is the age of your accounts, so closing an older account will cause the average age to rise and thus the potential to lower your score.

• You shouldn't pay off old debt and collections. This often causes your credit scores to go down. Paying them off triggers a new seven-year time period before credit bureaus remove negative items.

You or someone on your behalf should first attempt to negotiate a *pay for deletion* agreement whereby the collection agency or creditor is contacted in writing with an offer to pay in full or at a discount in exchange for deleting the account from your credit report.

On the other hand, your lender may want certain outstanding debts paid off at closing. You should discuss whether to pay off outstanding debts with your lender.

- Why do mortgage lenders pay so much attention to FICO scores?

   Statistics indicate a one in eight chance that a borrower with a FICO score below six hundred will prove either severely delinquent or default on a loan.

   A borrower with a score above eight hundred has a one in thirteen hundred chance of similar problems.

   Therefore, lenders rely on credit score evaluation systems.

- So what can you do to get and keep a higher score?

   First, make your payments on time.

   Second, refrain from applying for new credit.

   Third, try not to tap out credit.

- Where do you obtain your own credit reports and credit scores? Although there are many credit reporting agencies or credit bureaus, lenders tend to rely on three major US credit bureaus: Equifax, Experian, and TransUnion.

   Most mortgage companies will obtain your credit reports and credit scores with information merged from all three credit reporting agencies, a tri-merge credit report, at no cost to the potential borrower as part of a mortgage *pre-qualification*.

The procedure is quick, easy, and less expensive than to buy your credit report and credit score from each credit agency.

You can, however, obtain your credit reports for free and pay for your credit scores early if you aren't ready to meet with a lender to discuss getting a mortgage.

A federal law, the Fair and Accurate Credit Transactions Act of 2003—the FACT Act, requires that credit reporting agencies must provide one free credit report every twelve months.

The official web site is www.annualcreditreport.com.

Additional information can be found on the Federal Trade Commission's web site – www.ftc.gov. Click on the *Get Your Free Credit Report* button on the right side.

The free report doesn't include your credit score. Each credit bureau will charge extra for your credit score.

Thus getting your credit scores from a lender when you get pre-qualified at no cost may make more sense.

Caution: some credit scores offered by the credit repositories and others are called consumer scores and are not identical to what a lender requires or uses.

The Consumer Financial Protection Bureau, CFPB, recently took action against Experian and its subsidiaries for deceiving consumers about the use of credit scores it sold to consumers.

Experian claimed lenders used the credit scores to make credit decisions, but lenders didn't use Experian's scores for that purpose.

CFPB is a US government agency that makes sure banks, lenders, and other financial companies treat you fairly. The CFPB is an excellent source of information about credit and homebuying.

Navigate to the CFPB consumer website at www.consumerfinance.gov and check under *Consumer Tools* for more information about a number of financial related subjects.

At www.myfico.com/products/three-bureau-credit-report/, you can also obtain all three credit reports and FICO scores for all three for a one-time fee of about sixty dollars if you decide to check your credit and credit scores early.

The three major credit bureaus and their contact information are:

EQUIFAX
www.equifax.com 800-685-1111

EXPERIAN
www.experian.com 888-397-3742

TRANSUNION
www.transunion.com 800-888-4213

• Mortgage lenders request credit information from all three credit reporting agencies as well as your FICO scores as part of a mortgage application.

You should also.

Challenging Credit Report Errors

• Married couples should obtain individual reports rather than joint reports, as it is easier to challenge inaccurate information person by person.

It is also easier to challenge information on reports obtained separately from credit reporting agencies rather than from a combination report with information from two or three agencies.

Reports obtained at www.annualcreditreport.com are separate and thus easier to review and then, if necessary, challenge inaccurate information.

So if you got a combined tri-merge report from a lender you may want to follow that up with your individual reports at www.annualcreditreport.com so that challenging issues is easier to do.

- Depending on the nature of inaccurate information, you may want to start with the original vendor/ creditor before filing a challenge with the credit reporting agencies. Many medical collections are the result of improper filing with insurance companies by the doctor or hospital and thus need to be handled directly with them.

- If information is inaccurate or items clearly aren't yours, follow the next steps.

  Review reports and note inaccurate or unknown information. I recommend simply circling inaccurate items and noting what is wrong with the item, such as *not mine, unknown,* or *not accurate.*

  Then mail a hard copy of the report to the relevant reporting agencies and ask for *validation* of inaccurate items. Most people ask an agency to *verify* rather than *validate* the inaccurate information. It is easier for agencies to meet the legal threshold for *verification* than for *validation*. The law requires an agency to *validate*, so ask for *validation*.

  Send the original report with the notations on it via USPS Priority Mail so you have a receipt and record of when it arrived at the credit bureau. Keep a copy of the report before you mail it.

Go online to www.USPS.com and enter your tracking number to print out the notice that indicates delivery date.

Credit bureaus typically have a thirty to forty five day window for reviewing questioned items and reply about what they found and what action(s) they will take, such as removing or correcting the entry. Some situations may require several attempts to obtain an accurate report from each agency.

Credit reporting agencies are good at delay. If you want to have inaccuracies removed from your credit report, keep at it. Stick to your guns.

- What about negative information, such as bankruptcy, judgments, and collections?

Credit reporting agencies must remove bankruptcies from your credit report after ten years. They must remove judgments, collections, and other negative items after seven years, from date of last activity.

However, nothing in the law requires any negative item to remain for a minimum time. Many people believe that, if they have a bankruptcy or other negative item on the record, the consequence is a figurative credit prison for from seven to ten years.

If credit agencies report inaccurate information within an item that otherwise is accurate, however, you can legally challenge it. If the agencies can't validate the item and correct inaccurate information, they must remove the item.

Equifax, Experian, and TransUnion decided to remove new and existing tax-lien and civil-judgment data starting July 1, 2017, according to the Consumer Data Industry Association, a trade group that represents them. The firms will do so if the data doesn't include a list of at least three data points to insure accuracy: a person's name, address, and either a social security number or date of birth.

Many liens and most judgments don't include all three or four. Often bankruptcy records don't show accurate information either.

Sloppy Credit Bureau Practices

- A survey announced June 17, 2004, by The United States Public Interest Research Group (USPIRG) found:

One in four credit reports contains errors serious enough to cause consumers to be denied credit, a loan, an apartment or home loan or even a job. The big credit bureaus and big business tolerate big mistakes in credit reports," said Ed Mierzwinski, USPIRG Consumer Program Director. "But those mistakes ruin the financial reputations of hardworking Americans.

Over the last decade, the state PIRGs and other consumer organizations have issued numerous reports showing that sloppy credit bureau practices are at fault for errors in consumer credit reports.

"It is outrageous that inaccurate credit reports could damage one in four consumer's ability to buy a home, rent an apartment, obtain credit, open a bank account, or even get a job," said Mierzwinski.

USPIRG collected two hundred surveys from adults in thirty states who reviewed their credit reports for accuracy. Key findings include:

Twenty-five percent of the credit reports contained errors serious enough to result in the denial of credit

Seventy-nine percent of the credit reports contained mistakes of some kind

Fifty-four percent of the credit reports contained personal demographic identifying information that was misspelled, long-outdated, belonged to a stranger, or was otherwise incorrect

Thirty percent of the credit reports contained credit accounts that had been closed by the consumer but incorrectly remained listed as open.

• And according to a 2013 Federal Trade Commission study mandated by Congress, one in five consumers has an error in at least one of three major credit reports. The three credit bureaus received around eight million requests disputing information on credit reports in 2011, according to the Consumer Financial Protection Bureau (CFPB).

So, with a high percentage of credit reports containing mistakes of some kind, I think it makes sense to check your credit early in the process.

- What about credit repair companies?

  Although trying to get inaccurate information removed from your credit report(s) may take some time and patience, there is no reason to hire a credit repair company to do it for you.

  They are expensive to use and often not worth the cost.

  They will do the same things and follow the same procedures that you can on your own but charge you for it.

  The Consumer Financial Protection Bureau warns about how to tell a reputable credit counselor from a bogus credit repair company:

  There are counselors who can help you with your credit report, and others who take your money but don't help you. Warning signs for credit repair scams include companies that ask you to pay before providing services. The company may claim that it can guarantee a specific increase in your credit score or get rid of negative credit information in your credit report, even though the information is accurate and current.

  Additional information can be found at: www. consumerfinance.gov/ask-CFPB/how-can-I-tell-a-credit-repair-scam-from-a-reputable-credit-counselor-en-1343/

  Ask your lender or your *True Loyal Agent*™ to help you with the process. Certainly either has had other clients with such challenges, and they should be able to provide advice and assistance in your case.

Also, lenders sometimes have an expedited method to process directly to credit bureaus to speed up the process when there are obvious errors, so ask if your potential lender can help.

I've helped dozens of hopeful homebuyers improve their credit and credit scores. If you would like more information, go to www.tomwemett.com/credit-help.

Chapter Three
Understand Your Financing Options

Mortgage professionals can best assist with the difficult task of finding the ideal mortgage program.

They will review your resources: the three *Cs'* of homebuying:

- credit (based on the FICO credit score, discussed in *Chapter Two • Check and Improve Your Credit Scores)*

- cash flow (income vs debt payments)

- cash (available for down payment and closing costs)

Here, I will address cash flow and cash after presenting terms and options related to mortgage financing.

Based on your credit, cash flow (debt-to-income ratios), and cash available, a mortgage lender determines the right mortgage program as well as the mortgage amount likely to be approved.

It is important for you to know how much you can qualify for and/or be comfortable borrowing to determine the price range of property you should consider.

Knowing the mortgage amount a lender is likely to approve can help you determine if your goals are in line with reality. In other words, will you be comfortable with a home that you can afford to pay for?

Most people qualify for a much larger monthly mortgage payment than makes them comfortable.

It really is important, especially for first time homebuyers, that you to stay conservative and buy your first home with a comfortably affordable mortgage rather than end up house poor, as the saying goes.

Mortgage Programs

- Government-backed programs include those sponsored by the US government, such as the Federal Housing Administration (FHA), Veterans Administration (VA), and US Department of Agriculture (USDA) rural area loans. Some states also have their own mortgage programs.

  With government-backed programs, the government provides a guarantee to the lending institution as an inducement for them to lend money with lower down payments.

  Massachusetts hosts a couple of special mortgage programs.

  One Mortgage has several advantages. More info can be found at www.mhp.net/one-mortgage/why-one.

  The down payment is three percent for single family and two-family homes and five percent for three-family homes.

  The thirty-year fixed interest rate is discounted with no points paid and no private mortgage insurance (PMI), discussed later.

  Some income-eligible borrowers may qualify for additional monthly savings during the first seven years of the loan. Any home appreciation is yours and not shared with the program or lender.

One Mortgage is available only through banks and not through *mortgage brokers*. Not all banks participate in the program, so make sure to find out if your lender participates.

Other special loan programs are available through MassHousing, www.masshousing.com.

Features of a MassHousing loan include affordable interest rates fixed for the life of the loan; thirty-year repayment terms; mortgage payment protection that helps pay your loan in case you lose your job; no hidden fees or other surprises; low down-payment options; flexible underwriting and income limits with loans serviced by MassHousing.

While income limits based on household income for One Mortgage may disqualify potential homebuyers in urban areas including metropolitan Boston, MassHousing income limits are about double and based solely on the income of the borrower or borrowers and not on total household income.

- Other mortgage programs fall under the category of conventional loans.

Each type of conventional loan has unique qualifying requirements.

For example, federally chartered banks and lending institutions must reinvest a portion of funds into low- to moderate-income mortgages in their area of operation by providing Community Reinvestment Act (CRA) mortgages.

Such loans often have lower interest rates, lower down payments, grants to assist with down payments and closing costs, and more liberal qualifying requirements than other loans.

Private Mortgage Insurance (PMI)

Lending institutions often require PMI for conventional loans.

PMI protects a bank or lending institution in the event of a foreclosure when the buyer doesn't have at least a twenty-percent equity in the home.

Lending poses a greater risk when a buyer makes a down payment less than twenty percent.

The cost of PMI depends on your credit score and actual down payment. The higher the credit score and greater the down payment, the lower the cost of PMI.

Ask your lender to explain in more detail.

When the equity in the home reaches twenty-two percent of the original appraisal, the lender will automatically drop the PMI requirement, based on the amortization schedule that shows the balance of the mortgage after each payment.

However, if market value has increased based on general market factors or because of property improvements, you can ask the lender to consider dropping the PMI by requesting it and paying for a required new appraisal. If the equity is twenty-two percent or more, the lender should drop the PMI requirement.

Closing Cost Assistance

First-time homebuyers in Massachusetts will find down-payment and closing-cost-assistance programs and grants at: www.tomwemett.com/down-payment-resource.

The website links to an organization that maintains a database of down payment assistance programs throughout the country, including Massachusetts.

Enter the zip code of desired property plus additional qualifying information, and the site will match you with local programs.

Make a note of them and ask your potential lender if they participate in the programs.

Compare program possibilities with what the lender may offer.

When you meet with a lending institution representative, make sure that your potential lender knows about such programs and can check to see your eligibility for them.

First-Time Homebuyer Programs

Lenders generally consider a first-time homebuyer to be someone who has not owned a home in the previous three years.

If you have owned a home more than three years before approaching a lender, you could nevertheless qualify as a first-time homebuyer.

If you are considering taking advantage of a first-time homebuyer loan or grant, the lender will probably want to see your past three years of tax returns.

The lender will review the returns to see if you took a tax deduction for interest and real estate taxes on a home.

If you did so within the previous three years, you probably won't be eligible for a first-time homebuyer loan or assistance.

Lenders

- *Mortgage brokers* correspond with dozens of banks and lending institutions. *Mortgage brokers* do not fund a loan but rather act as mortgage originators on behalf of a financial institution or investor who holds the loan.

- *Mortgage bankers* are similar to a *mortgage brokers*. *Mortgage bankers* correspond with dozens of banks and lending institutions. They act as the mortgage originators. *Mortgage bankers*, however, fund loans and then resell or assign the loan to another person or institution.

- *Banks* and *savings and loan* associations (*S&Ls*) are local, regional, or national financial institutions where many people have checking or savings accounts. *Banks* and *S&Ls* generally originate, underwrite, and fund loans in-house but often sell your loan to other investors.

However, even if the *bank* or *S&L* sells your loan, it often retains the servicing in-house so that your payment will be made directly to the *bank* or *S&L* that originated your loan.

Some smaller *banks* and *S&Ls*, however, do not fund or service mortgages directly. Ask your potential lender for the extent of possible services.

- *Credit unions* are member-owned financial cooperatives democratically controlled by members and operated for the purpose of promoting thrift, providing credit at competitive rates, and providing other financial services to members. Many people belong to community *credit unions*.

  Credit unions often offer excellent mortgage and other loan options for their members, including many not available anywhere else.

  Credit unions typically originate, underwrite, fund, and service a loan in-house.

Payment Options

Mortgages also come with many payment options.

- The most widely used is a straight thirty-year fixed rate mortgage. Your monthly payment for principal and interest stays the same for the entire thirty-year period.

- Many lenders also offer a fifteen or twenty year fixed rate mortgage. The payment will be higher as you are paying the loan back in a shorter period of time but these will also save you interest.

- Other options include adjustable rate mortgages (known as ARMs).

  If you know that you plan to stay in a home only for from three to five years, perhaps a 3/1 or 5/1 ARM would be appropriate for your situation.

  The rate will likely be slightly lower to begin with but can adjust after the three-year or five-year term, likely up, depending on the prime lending rate.

  Generally, rates go up when the term rolls over, but if you plan to sell and move before the change in rate, you can save money.

  However, a decline in the real estate market could make selling a property before the rate adjusts impractical as your home's value may have declined so you can't or don't want to sell.

  Then, you may end up staying in the home and paying a higher interest rate and monthly payment due to the ARM's interest rate adjusting yearly.

- Another option is to pay points to lower the interest rate. One point is one percent of the mortgage amount. One point on a hundred-thousand-dollar mortgage is one thousand dollars.

  Your lender's representative should be able to explain and suggest any of these alternatives if appropriate for your situation.

- You also generally have the option of prepaying your mortgage to save interest and paying it off sooner.

One such option is called a bi-weekly mortgage payment that results in your paying one extra month payment over a year's time period that often shortens the length of time to paying off the loan from thirty years to twenty years and dramatically reducing the total interest paid.

Check to make sure that the mortgage you get doesn't have a prepayment penalty and that however you want to make extra payments you aren't penalized for doing so.

Another option: rather than obtaining a twenty-year fixed rate mortgage that requires a commitment to a higher payment, you may want to obtain a thirty-year fixed rate mortgage.

When you have some extra cash, make an extra payment to be applied to principal along with your regular payment.

Contact the lender to find out the best way to make an extra payment.

If you pay by coupon, sometimes the coupon will have a place to write in the amount of an extra payment.

Often, however, it won't.

If the coupon doesn't, you should pay the mortgage payment with one check and then pay the extra amount in a separate check with a notation that the extra payment should be applied to principal.

Unless clearly directed, lenders may apply an extra payment to the escrow account for taxes and insurance rather than apply it toward principal.

If the extra payment is not applied to principal, the payment will not reduce the mortgage balance nor your overall interest amount.

Cash-Flow Requirements

Determining the amount of a mortgage you can qualify for is generally figured by applying debt-to-income ratios.

As a rule of thumb, conventional financing requires a debt-to-income ratio of 28/36.

FHA and other forms of financing have their own requirements, often more liberal than 28/36.

The first ratio, twenty-eight percent in our example, is the maximum percentage of your gross monthly income that the bank will allow you for your total monthly mortgage payment, known as *PITI*, including:
- **P**rincipal—the amount you pay back to the bank every month)
- **I**nterest—the profit to the bank each month
- Real Estate **T**axes—the real estate property taxes due for your home in your local area
- Homeowners **I**nsurance—your fire and liability insurance on your home and *PMI*, if applicable.

The second ratio, thirty six percent in our example, is the maximum percentage of your gross monthly income that the bank will allow you for the above total monthly mortgage payment PLUS your other monthly debt payments.

The lender's representative can explain qualifying ratios in more detail and provide examples for you based on your specific information.

Cash Requirements

What about cash for a down payment and closing costs and escrows for taxes and insurance? You should have some cash saved up and sitting in a checking or savings account.

Even a no-down-payment loan requires some cash for closing costs and escrow for taxes and insurance.

Make sure that you don't just stick a bunch of cash into your account that you can't document. Some people save up cash but don't place it in an account until they are ready to buy a home.

Perhaps you worked "under the table" or sold some items on eBay or in a yard sale. These are hard to document. Such cash has to be "seasoned," that is it must be in your bank account at least for between sixty and ninety days prior to applying for a mortgage.

Otherwise you will need to prove the source of any recent cash deposits outside of your regular pay checks.

For example, if a relative gives you cash, it must be documented and some loan programs have restrictions on how much cash you can be given for a home purchase or they require a signed statement from your relative that it is a gift and not a loan.

What are some other potential sources of cash besides your savings?

- Do you have any assets you could sell and raise some additional cash? Do you have a car, a boat, or a snowmobile you could part with in order to buy a home? Perhaps you have a stamp or coin collection that might make sense to sell.

- Do you have a relative who could loan or is willing to make a gift to you of money to help out? You never know.

  Let your relatives know that you are contemplating a purchase, and one of them may be willing to help.

  If a relative is willing to loan rather than make a gift to you of money, you may be required to have the relative sign a bank document certifying that the money is not a loan but rather a gift, as lenders generally do not allow loans from other sources for the down payment.

  If your relative loans you money, you should make arrangements to pay your relative according to mutually agreed-upon terms.

- Getting married soon? Instead of people giving you toasters, ask that they help with a cash contribution toward a down payment and closing costs for a home instead.

You can buy whatever appliances or other such items after the closing on the home.

- Are you a valuable employee with a smaller company? See if the company will contribute money toward your home purchase.

I had a client who was a very valuable employee with his company. He mentioned he planned to buy a home, and his company gave him a bonus of five thousand dollars.

My client had to pay taxes on the bonus, but after taxes, it remained a nice surprise and helped out in his being able to find the right home.

- Do you qualify for special down payments or closing costs/escrows for taxes and insurance programs? Check www.tomwemett.com/down-payment-resource for a link to a website that provides information on such programs.

Mortgage Qualifying Letter

What is a mortgage *pre-approval* or *pre-qualification?* Mortgage *pre-approval* or *pre-qualification* certifies your financial viability through a *qualifying letter* issued to you after you have contacted a lender and provided requested financial information.

The letter will state the purchase price you qualify for, the down payment you plan to make, and the loan program you plan to accept.

Show the letter when you make an offer on a home to inform the seller and seller's agent that you have met with a prospective lender and are likely to qualify for a loan sufficient to buy the property.

When you agree to buy a home, the seller will take it off the market for from forty-five to sixty days in most cases while the buyer applies for mortgage financing.

The seller and seller's agent don't want to hear forty-five days into the deal that you can't get a mortgage.

Knowing in advance that you have pre-qualified reassures the seller and seller's agent, thus providing peace of mind, that you will be able to complete the transaction on time.

Before the Consumer Financial Protection Bureau (CFPB) put regulations in place for lenders on October 3, 2015, the lending community considered *pre-qualification* the personal opinion of a lender about what a person would qualify for, based on information given a lending institution by the potential borrower.

The lender typically did not request a full tri-merge credit report with FICO scores or attempt to verify income, employment, or assets.

Pre-approval, on the other hand, formerly meant a mortgage commitment subject to having a property under contract and the property's appraising for at least the purchase price.

Pre-approval was usually based on a review of a tri-merge credit report and FICO scores along with verification of employment and income by means of copies of pay stubs and income tax returns and verification of assets by means of copies of bank statements and other documentation.

Pre-approval required a more involved, accurate, and reliable process thus more desirable to potential sellers and agents.

Since October 3, 2015, the terms *pre-qualification* and *pre-approval* are generally used interchangeably.

Some lenders even believe that new regulations prohibit them from using the term *pre-approval.*

Today, *qualifying letters* rarely carry much weight, although there are steps you can take to help your *qualifying letter* make a good impression on the seller and the seller's agent.

Whether the lender's *qualifying letter* is called a *pre-qualification* or *pre-approval* letter doesn't matter. Nevertheless, it should state:

This pre-qualification is based on my review of a tri-merge credit report and FICO scores as well as verification of employment and income by means of copies of pay stubs and other documentation and verification of assets by means of copies of bank statements and other documentation.

If the *qualifying letter* doesn't include the above verbiage or verbiage that means something similar, the seller and seller's agent may wonder if the relevant information had been scrutinized.

Adding the suggested language lets the seller and seller's agent know that the lender took extra steps to verify your credit, income, and assets and that the *qualifying letter* has some basis for the information presented and, thus, is stronger.

If you are competing with other buyers who simply obtain standard letters and you provide one that contains something similar to the language I've noted above, your offer may receive greater consideration.

Meet with several prospective lenders initially not to get a *qualifying letter* but to learn about mortgage products and to ask lenders about their processes for providing a *qualifying letter*.

You want a lender who will obtain a full tri-merge credit report and FICO scores, who will verify your employment and income with pay stubs and income tax returns, and who will verify your assets by reviewing copies of your bank statements and other financial documentation.

If a prospective lender doesn't do a thorough review of your financial situation, the lender won't be able to provide you with a strong *qualifying letter*, and you should find another lender. I have a local lender who won't do a thorough check and thus can provide only what amounts to what we used to call a *pre-qualification* that would leave you in a weaker negotiation position.

I won't recommend the particular bank due to the policy about *qualifying letter*s, as I don't want to put my buyer clients into such a weak position.

If the lender will gather and review information as noted, ask for a copy of the *qualifying letter*.

If the above language or something similar isn't in the letter, provide sample language and ask if the prospective lender will add it to the letter should you decide to seek a loan from the lender.

Many lenders, anxious for your business, will comply. After all, you are asking the lender to put in writing what the lender has verified and checked prior to writing the letter.

New mortgage regulations do not prohibit lenders from including the language I provide above.

Still, as a routine practice, lenders don't seem to want to include the language. Don't be afraid to ask for inclusion of the language in a *qualifying letter*—or consider using another lender who will.

Loan Estimate

What is a *loan estimate* and why do you need one?

The CFPB requires an official *loan estimate* according to a rule that went into effect on October 3, 2015 as part of regulations overseen by the Consumer Financial Protection Bureau – www.cfpb.gov.

The lender provides the official *loan estimate* on a standardized form with important information, including the estimated interest rate, monthly payment, and total closing costs for the loan.

The official *loan estimate* also gives you information about the estimated costs of taxes and insurance, and how the interest rate and payments may change in the future. The form uses clear language and is designed to help you better understand the terms of the mortgage loan you've applied for.

The official *loan estimate* must be provided to you within three business days of receiving your application for a mortgage.

The official *loan estimate*, however, is not used when obtaining a *qualifying letter.* Instead, a prospective lender should give you an informal estimate of closing costs so you have an idea of what costs and fees are due at closing. Then, you can plan accordingly.

Find more information about the official *loan estimate* at www.consumerfinance.gov/owning-a-home/loan-estimate.

Annual Percentage Rate

What is APR, the annual percentage rate?

The APR is a way to compare the actual costs of different loans.

If you have two loans offering the same interest rate but different closing costs the APR computation will show a higher figure for the loan with the higher closing costs

For example, a loan might have a note rate of 4.5% but an APR of 4.75%. You would make a payment based on 4.5%, but the APR of 4.75% gives you a way of comparing one loan to another.

If the second loan you are considering has higher closing costs, the APR for the second loan could be 4.90%. By comparing, you have the idea that the first loan probably is the better deal.

The APR computation is especially useful if you have two loans showing different interest rates and closing costs.

For example, the first loan may have a 4.5% note rate but an APR of 4.9% while the second loan may have a 4.65% note rate but an APR of 4.75% making it the better loan to get.

The APR computation isn't perfect, but it does give you a basis for comparing loans.

Chapter Four

Set Realistic Goals

Once you have a clear understanding of your financing options and the price range you can afford given your resources, the next item of business is to have a clear idea of your needs and wants about a home in order to set realistic goals.

Too many buyers just go out looking at homes without a clear understanding of what they are looking for.

Also, you must keep in mind that you will sell at some point in the future. What features of the home that appeal to you may not appeal to future buyers?

Be very careful not to buy in the extreme to the point that you will have difficulty selling in the future.

I recommend that you list specifics of what you need and what you think you want, making a distinction between the two categories.

List features that would be considered pluses and, separately, features that would be considered minuses.

If more than one person is involved in the purchase, I suggest that each of you do your own list and then compare and combine into one list.

Start with Basics

- How big a home do you want? What square footage? Do you know what twelve hundred square feet looks like? How big is your current residence?

  Remember that you have to pay heating and cooling costs and clean and maintain the home. The larger the home, the higher potential costs to heat, cool, clean, or maintain.

- How many bedrooms? Do you need one or more guest rooms? Maybe a hobby room? I have one of our spare bedrooms as a model train room. Do you need a sewing or craft room?

  Bedrooms aren't just for sleeping, so you should take into consideration potential or alternative uses.

  Also, looking ahead when you sell the home, would one or two bedrooms be sufficient to appeal to enough buyers or would a three-plus bedroom home attract more buyers in the future?

- How many bathrooms? How many people will live in the home, and can one bathroom meet your needs? Will there be times when more than one person has to use a bathroom and, thus, two full baths or one bath with another half bath may be more of a need than a want?

  Do you have a need for a tub? Some people like showers and can live without a tub.

But what about whoever buys the home from you? Having a tub/shower combination appeals to more future buyers than a simple shower.

- How large a garage? How many bays in the garage for cars? How much stuff do you need to store in the garage?

  Many garages end up without room for a car due to storage needs.

  Can you do with a one-car garage? Will it be sufficient for a vehicle plus storage of a lawn mower, garden tools, and bikes?

  Can you add a storage building somewhere to relieve the garage of storage so that a one-car garage may be sufficient?

- What style of home? Homes come in all sorts of styles. However, remember that what appeals to you may not appeal to buyers in the future when you go to sell.

  Contemporary homes look great in a magazine and even in person, but are they practical for everyday living and will the style of the home limit potential buyers in the future?

- What general location? Do you like an urban setting where you can walk to almost anything you want or take urban transportation easily for shopping or entertainment? Check out www.walkscore.com to see how an address rates in terms of proximity to shopping and entertainment.

Do you like a more rural setting? We have beehives and a garden and, thus, like our rural setting. However, we are car dependent.

When considering location, remember that prices tend to be much higher the closer in a home is to urban centers, such as Boston. If you work and play in Boston, for example, you may need to check out suburban areas that are served by mass transit into Boston in order to find a home you can afford.

The more rural you go, the lower prices tend to be. Also, some mortgage loan programs from agencies like USDA, US Department of Agriculture, are available only in rural areas.

- What age of home? Some older homes seem to have amazing charm. They just don't make or design homes like they used to.

  But, what is the condition of the older home? Has the electric been updated? Has the plumbing been updated? Has the septic been updated?

  How much work does the home need? Does it need cosmetic updates? Does it have structural or mechanical issues that will cost you a lot of money to update and/or to maintain?

- What school district? Check out: www.greatschools. org/schools/cities/Massachusetts/MA/ for information about Massachusetts schools.

While school rankings are important, I think it is more important to visit schools and talk to administrators, teachers, and parents of children in school.

Get a feel for the learning atmosphere in the school district where you may buy a home.

Also, you may already have your children in a school district and want to remain in that district. Your agent can search for homes you may want to buy based on the school district you prefer.

Consider Other Options

- Swimming pool? Swimming pools are a mixed bag. Some people love them, and others hate them.

  Pools can be expensive to maintain, and they occasion the issue of increased liability and need for a safety fence or other preventive measures to restrict access.

  What if you don't want a pool but you find the otherwise perfect home with an above-ground pool. Do you skip it or do what one of my clients did?

  She posted a notice at work that she would have an above-ground pool for sale for four hundred dollars. She pre-sold it in one day.

- Fenced yard? Do you have young children? Do you have a dog? You may want a fenced yard but could add one if needed including an Invisible Fence™ for dogs.

- Fireplace? Fireplaces require increased maintenance and mean safety concerns. Yes, you may have the idea that it would be nice to curl up in front of a fireplace on a cold winter night, but ask yourself about the condition of the chimney.

Does the chimney need a liner to prevent chimney fires if the chimney has deteriorated or cracked to the point of letting ashes and hot embers into the structure of the home?

When was the chimney last cleaned? Fireplace chimneys should be cleaned and inspected at least once per season.

Will a fireplace increase the cost of your insurance?

Would a pellet stove be more practical or perhaps a wood burning-stove or pellet stove insert for the fireplace?

- Finished basement? If the basement isn't already finished and you really want to accomplish the task, is the ceiling height sufficient to add a dropped ceiling?

Is the basement dry enough to finish? If there are moisture issues, be sure to address them before adding improvements to the basement.

What about radon in the home? Even though nearby homes don't have radon your prospective home may have elevated levels of radon.

If you are going to finish the basement, make sure to have it checked for radon as part of the contingency process in your offer. If the test shows elevated radon levels, it is much less expensive to have a radon mitigation system installed before the basement is finished and possibly the seller will pay for the mitigation system as part of negotiation of repairs.

Is there more than one means of ingress and egress from the basement? Many building or health codes require at least two methods of ingress and egress if the basement space is finished off and you want to use it as additional living space.

Check on building codes to make sure that any already finished basement meets codes or that any planned improvements meet codes. Properly finished basements usually add to the value of a home.

- Air Conditioning? Massachusetts does experience high temperatures from time to time. Does the home have good airflow to the extent that air conditioning isn't necessary?

  Does the home have a forced air heating system allowing air conditioning to be easily added?

  If the home has a boiler or hot water heating system, air conditioning will have to be a separate system or window air conditioning may do the job.

- Hardwood floors? Are they in good shape? Some people appreciate hardwood floors while others do not like them. How do you feel about them?

Do you prefer carpet? Perhaps wood floors with throw rugs will work for you.

- Porch and/or Deck? We can all appreciate the picture of sitting outside with a drink in hand enjoying the evening.

  Is a deck or porch a plus or a real need in order to have a place to relax? Can a porch or deck be added?

Another idea is to list reasons why a feature is important to you. For example, you may desire three bedrooms. Yet, you may intend to use one so-called bedroom as a den or office.

Perhaps a two-bedroom home with a separate den-office would meet your needs.

Go through the variables in this chapter, respond to each question, and then ask yourself *why* you have provided each response in order to dig deeper to ascertain how important each feature is to you.

Needs vs Wants

It is important that you separate needs from wants. For example, you may want a two-car garage but only need a one-car garage.

The two-car garage could be a real plus in your mind, but if the home with a one-car garage meets your other needs, it may end up being the available home you most desire. After all, you might be able to expand the garage into a two-car garage in the future.

Another example would be the desire or want to have a half bath on the first floor. Often there is space on the first floor, such as an extra closet or a bump-out into the garage where a half-bath could be installed. So even if a home doesn't have the half bath you prefer, you may decide that a home without it is your best choice.

Caution

You should keep your options as open as possible. If you restrict your search to the ideal home, you may not have many options to choose from, and you may become frustrated and stressed out with the process.

Buyers should stay flexible in order to have a sufficient number of homes to consider. Search on the minimum of features you consider absolute musts. Stay flexible on the rest.

The ideal home probably doesn't exist, but many homes will come close if you remain flexible.

Also, the ideal home may not be within your price range at the moment but could be in your price range as time passes.

You should be realistic about what you are about to purchase. It is easy to get carried away with what you think you want. It is understandable. We constantly see pictures of fancy homes in magazines and online.

However, it is important for you to remain in touch with reality. Sometimes a home is out of your reach at the present time.

It is important to understand that the home you purchase probably isn't the last home that you will ever own.

It is better to buy wisely and within your means.

Goals vs Reality

Once you are comfortable with financing options, have an understanding of what you are willing to pay, and have a good minimum idea about features and options, your next step is to see if your ideas line up with one another.

- Do so by checking out homes for sale. You can check easily on the internet these days *without calling a real estate licensee.*

  You are not ready to interface with a real estate agent at this point unless the person is the right agent as described in *Chapter Five • Find and Work with a True Loyal Agent*^{TM}.

  To find homes for sale in Massachusetts go to: www.tomwemett.com/mass-homes-for-sale. The link will take you to the Massachusetts MLS Property Information Network (MLSPIN) for access to all REALTOR® listings statewide.

  Go to www.realtor.com for the best up-to-date, comprehensive database of listed property anywhere else in the country.

- **WARNING:** Do not give out your email address, phone number, or other contact information. To do so will invite aggressive sales tactics by traditional real estate industry *licensees-salespeople.*

Realtor.com and other online listing sites such as Trulia and Zillow make their money by selling your information as leads for real estate *salespeople*.

Local real estate company websites also attempt to get yourself to leave your contact information for that company's agents to follow-up on.

Getting your name and contact information also provides the real estate *licensees* who receive them as a way potentially to say you are their buyer.

In a possibility I will discuss later, a real estate agent you contact on the internet may claim they are due a commission in the event you buy any home they informed you about.

Guard your confidential information closely.

• Do homes in your price range appear to have features and options that you want?

If not, then you may need to reconsider your homebuying decision.

You may have to wait for another year to build up more money for a larger down payment.

You may require time to improve your credit score so you can obtain a lower interest rate which would allow you to buy a more expensive home.

You may have to pay off more debt so you can afford a larger monthly payment.

You may need to adjust your features list and consider a less ideal home.

Save yourself time, effort, and heartache.

Make sure your needs are in line with your financial abilities.

Be realistic, and you will feel much better about your homebuying adventure.

- If two or more of you will make the decision, get on the same page and stay there.

I've had couples look at certain homes, and right away, I knew they did not think along the same lines. I had to review their needs and wants list with them to find common ground between them.

The review saved much time and effort as they looked at homes.

- Sometimes, however, one person will dominate search criteria and the choice of homes we look at.

You may regret buying a home that one party likes and the other doesn't.

I had a couple that wanted to buy a fixer-upper. After the transaction closed, I learned that *he* wanted the fixer-upper but *she* wanted a ready-to-move-into-home.

She blamed me for pushing them into a fixer-upper. He dominated the process, and she suffered.

- It is best to find common ground and compromises, or you shouldn't buy a home and continue renting.

  At least with renting, your commitment amounts to one year or less. Buying a home usually comes with a commitment to a thirty-year mortgage.

  Without taking a big financial hit, it usually isn't easy to sell a home within a year or two because you decide the home doesn't meet your needs.

- If you are a dating couple and think it would be great to own a home together, make sure you really are ready for the financial commitment of borrowing money together to buy a home.

  I've had clients who decided to split up just as we processed a contract to purchase a home.

  They tried to use the home inspection contingency to get out of the contract, but the home had nothing sufficiently wrong to warrant their doing that. They refused to go through with the home purchase and lost their contract deposit.

  Rather than face such a loss, rent for a while and make sure that living together and paying joint bills works before you buy a home and take on a thirty-year mortgage commitment together instead of a month-to-month or one-year lease obligation.

Chapter Five
Find and Work with a
True Loyal Agent™

Once you have selected homes to look at, especially online, you are ready to go to the actual home and look at it physically.

Online listings and what you read and see online often depend on exaggeration. Creative photos, homes that have been staged, and nice descriptions may not provide an accurate account of the home.

- Before you start calling listing agents to see homes, you must understand how doing so may harm you.

  You must find the right agent to accompany you as you see homes, and it will not to be among the listing agents for the homes you found online.

  After all, they represent sellers.

- It probably will not be a real estate *licensee-salesperson* referred to you by a relative, neighbor, friend, or co-worker. They probably didn't use the right agent or know about *True Loyal Agents*™. In fact—thinking they were properly represented when they weren't—they may have used a *fake* buyer's agent.

  Therefore, following the advice of a relative, neighbor, friend, or co-worker may not be the best way to go about buying a home.

- Also, be leery of online testimonials.

First, the real estate *licensee* someone refers you to may not be a true agent.

Chances are a referrer may not realize that true agents exist or what the difference is between a *salesperson* and a true agent.

Second, testimonials can be staged. I've known of instances of fake positive testimonials uploaded to make someone look good and fake negative testimonials uploaded to make someone look bad.

Third, who is going to post negative testimonials about themselves? Reviews you find on a real estate *licensee*'s website will be positive.

I'm not saying that testimonials aren't valuable. You just have to consider their source. And, more importantly, you must consider whether or not they are about a *True Loyal Agent*™ as described in this book.

You should start working with the right agent as early as possible in the homebuying process.

The right agent is one who really is a *True Loyal Agent*™ who has the legal obligation to be your protector, be loyal to you alone, and look out for your best interest at all times and in every situation.

As mentioned in *Introduction • Who Can You Really Trust?*, I've coined the name *True Loyal Agent*™ to refer to a real estate *licensee*/true agent who is with a company that represents real estate consumers as a true agent and never practices *dual agency or designated agency*, explained later in this chapter.

A *True Loyal Agent™* is always loyal and always a true agent.

True Loyal Agents™ provide full fiduciary duties at all times and in every situation. The practice is the mark of a true agent. You are the client, also known as the principal. They are your agent.

Fiduciary duties owed to you by such an agent are known by the acronym **OLDCAR.**

- **O**bedience to Lawful Instruction
- Undivided **L**oyalty
- Full **D**isclosure of Material Information
- **C**onfidentiality
- **A**ccountability
- **R**easonable Skill and Care

A *True Loyal Agent™* will protect you from making mistakes outlined in the previous four chapters as well as mistakes discussed later.

True Loyal Agents™ who represent homebuyers only are known as *exclusive buyer agents*.

True Loyal Agents™ who may represent buyers and sellers but never both in the same transaction are known as *true single-party agents*.

I'll discuss these types of agents in more detail below and tell you how to find them.

So before I continue my discussion, I suggest that you stop right now, write the following statement on a piece of paper, and sign it.

Doing so may be the most important thing you do to avoid being sold the wrong home and being taken advantage of.

If there are two people buying, both of you should sign the statement.

You have the right to remain silent. Anything you say can and will be used against you! You should not assume that any real estate broker or salesperson represents you unless you agree to engage a real estate licensee in an authorized brokerage relationship whereby the licensee guarantees to be loyal to you and be your true agent at all times and in every situation and not to downgrade representation of you to dual agent or designated agent. You are advised not to disclose any information you want to be held in confidence until you make a decision on representation. Your signature below acknowledges your understanding and acceptance of this statement.

Your Options

Homebuyers in Massachusetts can choose to work with real estate *licensees* who represent the seller, real estate *licensees* who represent the buyer, real estate *licensees* who try to represent both the seller and the buyer (known in Massachusetts as *dual agents* or *designated agents*), or real estate *licensees* who represent neither the seller nor the buyer (known in Massachusetts as *facilitators*).

Real estate *licensees* who represent the seller, by law, must be loyal to the seller and must look out for the seller's best interest and work to get the highest price and best terms for the seller.

Real estate *licensees* who represent the buyer, by law, must be loyal to the buyer and must look out for the buyer's best interest and work to get the lowest price and best terms for the buyer.

Real estate *licensees—dual agents or designated agents*—who attempt to work for both must remain neutral and really can't provide either party the **OLD** part of our acronym noted above:

- **O**bedience to Lawful Instruction
- Undivided **L**oyalty
- Full **D**isclosure.

However, in Massachusetts, the Mandatory Real Estate Licensee-Consumer Relationship Disclosure form implies that *designated agents* can provide *undivided loyalty*.

Common sense tells you something isn't quite right with a so-called *designated agent* being able to provide *undivided loyalty* to you when one or more other agents in the same real estate company are saying the same thing to the seller of the home you want to buy.

Agents who work both sides have ongoing relationships with one another. Can you trust that their loyalty to you and your home purchase is greater than their loyalty to their office and coworkers?

You want the lowest price and best terms, and the seller wants the highest price and best terms.

And the real estate company wants to make a deal and double-end a commission from both the sell side and buy side of the transaction and often will pay a higher commission split to its agents for an in-house sale.

In an effort to make an in-house sale, traditional real estate *licensees-salespeople* share information all the time about their buyers' and sellers' needs and qualifications.

They do so in passing or at sales meetings or over lunch or coffee.

Do you believe it is to your advantage to have a *licensee-salesperson* telling others in their company they have a qualified buyer and then sharing with them how much you are qualified to pay or that you have cash for a sizable down payment or that your lease is up in two months and you have to move quickly?

Do you think the information won't be used against you?

Do you believe that they can somehow properly represent you as buyer on an in-house sale?

Do you believe there is no chance you will be short-changed?

I can get into great detail as to why *designated agency* is not proper and has no true legal basis to operate as purported.

However, I will simply leave it up to your good sense and judgment here and say that agreeing to *dual agency* or *designated agency* could cost you thousands of dollars.

This chapter is about finding a *True Loyal Agent*™ who takes all the uncertainty out of knowing whether or not the real estate agent you use really is a *True Loyal Agent* or really a *salesperson* in disguise pretending to be your agent.

Relationships you have with an attorney or a CPA are based on trust law.

Attorneys and CPAs are required by law to be loyal to you and look out for your best interest at all times.

They are your fiduciary and your agent, and you are their client.

They owe the full range of **OLDCAR** fiduciary duties to you that I mentioned above when describing a *True Loyal Agent*™.

I'd like to impress on you the importance of true *undivided loyalty* and what it means.

Undivided loyalty prohibits an agent or real estate *licensee* from advancing any interests adverse to your own.

Such loyalty is undivided because it takes only you and your welfare into account.

A true buyer's agent cannot advance interests of the seller or themselves or their real estate company above yours.

The fiduciary duty of *undivided loyalty* is impossible for agents to provide if they or their company practices *dual agency* or *designated agency* and you are buying a home listed by the same agent or another agent in the same company.

A real estate *licensee* can function as a true fiduciary just like your attorney or CPA or can function as merely a *salesperson*, or worse, a make-believe, *fake* buyer's agent.

The situation provides probably the most confusing aspect of dealing with a real estate *licensee* in Massachusetts.

Are you dealing with someone who is a fiduciary and who you can trust or someone who is a *salesperson* whom you need to guard against?

Adding to the confusion, real estate *licensees* are called *agents*, when in most instances they really aren't your agent but rather an agent for the seller or simply not an agent at all but rather a *salesperson*.

To reduce confusion, I like to refer to them as *salespersons* or *licensees* rather than agents.

Of course, the decision is up to you.

My role is to let you know that there are real estate *licensees* who believe with a passion in true loyal representation. Such *licensees* reject the deeply ingrained sales culture of the traditional real estate industry, the double-dipping of commissions, as well as *dual agency* or *designated agency.*

They *guarantee* their *undivided loyalty* to you regardless of which property you are interested in buying.

Other real estate *licensees* can't do that.

As a result, working with a traditional real estate industry *licensee-salesperson* may cause doubt at times as to the *licensee*'s motives or actions.

Working with what I refer to as a *True Loyal Agent*™ removes all doubt with regard to the *licensee*'s loyalty and dedication to getting you the best deal on the right home.

I'm assuming you don't want to be sold a home, especially one that is not best for you.

But rather you want to buy a home with someone who is truly on your side and who has a legal obligation to be loyal to you and look out for your best interest at all times and in every situation.

You should therefore seek the services of a real estate *licensee* who really is your agent and who will guarantee to be loyal to you, who will protect you, and who will look out for your best interest no matter which property you are interested in.

In other words, you want a *True Loyal Agent*™ to represent you.

If you decide to buy a home while working with an agent who represents the seller or is operating as a *dual agent* or *designated agent*, you will end up buying your home working with a *salesperson* just as you do when buying a used car.

Who is the better advocate for your best deal?

An agent who represents the seller?

Agents in the same company who try to represent both you and the seller?

Or an agent who will represent only you in a transaction?

As mentioned above, the right agent that works best for homebuyers in Massachusetts and elsewhere, for that matter, is an *exclusive buyer's agent* or a *true single-party agent.*

You should be able to discern why after reading each agent's description.

Exclusive Buyer's Agents

True *exclusive buyer's agents* never take listings, never represent sellers, and don't work for a company that does. They never operate as *dual agents* or *designated agents* or *facilitators.* They represent and protect buyers only as *True Loyal Agents*™ at all times and in every situation.

Single-Party Agents

True single-party agents work for buyers and sellers, but never both in the same transaction, and never operate as *dual agents* or *designated agents* or *facilitators. True single-party agents* and *single-party agency offices* follow procedures to make sure that their buyer and seller clients will never be represented by the firm at the same time.

They will always refer the seller or buyer to another competent agent outside their firm rather than try to represent both a buyer and seller in the same transaction as traditional real estate companies do as their routine business model.

For example, before *true single-party agents* will take you on as a buyer client, they will first make sure that none of their current listings interest you.

If one or more of their listed properties interest you, they will not be able to take you on as a client.

They will refer you to someone outside of their firm to represent you if that is what you would like, or you could continue to purchase their listing as a customer, not a client and without representation.

I don't recommend that you go it alone or even alone with the help of an attorney. Get true representation, and then continue.

If you have no interest in any of the firm's current listings then the firm can take you on as a true client with the firm as your *True Loyal Agent*™.

If you are already a buyer client of a *single-party real-estate agency* and a seller approaches the firm with a home to list, the firm will check to see if it is a home you might be interested in buying.

If so, they won't take on the seller as a client but rather encourage the seller to find someone else to list with or sell as a "for sale by owner," perhaps working with an attorney for help.

If you wish to continue with a purchase of that home, the firm continues fully representing you.

A *true single-party agent* operates as a *True Loyal Agent*™ at all times and in every situation and operates similar to a law firm.

A law firm represents sellers and buyers of real estate but never in the same transaction.

If a law firm had a previous relationship with a seller, the law firm would not be able to represent a buyer vs that seller in a subsequent transaction.

I referred a buyer client to an attorney who handles real estate transactions for my buyer clients.

I had to find a different attorney with a different law firm because someone else in the law firm had ten years previously represented the child of the seller from whom my buyer client intended to buy a home.

Note that the attorney to whom I referred my buyer client was not directly involved in the previous matter, but because someone else in the law firm had been involved, the attorney to whom I wanted to refer the business had to recuse himself.

How do you know if you are talking to a *True Loyal Agent*™ in Massachusetts?

Ask the real estate *licensee-salesperson* if the *licensee-salesperson* or anyone else in their company takes listings. If the *licensee-salesperson* or someone else in the company takes listings, the real estate *licensee* you have asked is not an *exclusive buyer's agent* or with an *exclusive buyer agency.*

However, the *licensee-salesperson* may still be a *True Loyal Agent™.* You have to ask the next question to see if the *licensee* is a *true-single-party agent.*

Ask if the *licensee-salesperson* will refer you out to someone else with another real estate company if you are interested in a home listed by them or someone else in their company.

If the *licensee* won't refer you out and claims it is possible to represent both the seller and you as the buyer, the agent is not a *true single-party agent.*

If you continue working with such an agent, you could end up with the potential of being pushed into buying an in-house listing and ending up in a *dual agency* or *designated agency* situation, which could harm you.

How do you find a *True Loyal Agent™* in Massachusetts?
You should always interview a true *exclusive buyer's agent* or a *true single-party agent* before deciding to work with an agent. It costs you nothing extra to learn what such an agent does and how such an agent guarantees to be your loyal agent regardless of which property you end up buying.

It is possible that you received a copy of this book from a *True Loyal Agent™* in Massachusetts, and therefore, you already have a *True Loyal Agent™* working for you. If not, find a *True Loyal Agent™* in Massachusetts by contacting the

Massachusetts Association of Buyer Agents (MABA), online at www.massbuyeragents.org or by calling 800-935-6222. All MABA members are either *true exclusive buyer agent*s or *true single-party agents* and thus are *True Loyal Agent*s™.

If you happen to be a seller reading this book, your best option is to work with a *true single-party agency*. It is the best way for you to be fully represented throughout the home selling process.

Contact the Massachusetts Association of Buyer Agents, MABA, and say you are a seller and would like to talk to a *single-party agent* to sell your home. MABA will direct you to a *true single-party agent* to help you.

More Tips about Working with Agents

- Always ask any real estate *licensee* to provide you with a copy of a completed Massachusetts Mandatory Real Estate Licensee-Consumer Relationship Disclosure before you provide any information to the *licensee* or see any homes in company with that *licensee*.

  Get the completed disclosure at your first contact with the *licensee*, even though the disclosure isn't mandatory until you actually discuss a specific property.

  Of course it probably would be too late by then as you would have provided confidential information to the *licensee* in the meantime and thus put yourself at a great disadvantage.

You should know if the *licensee* will operate as a *True Loyal Agent™* or a *dual agent* or *designated agent*. You do not have to sign the disclosure and, even if you do, it is not a contract.

A copy of the disclosure can be found here: www.tomwemett.com/disclosure.

The disclosure states that it is not a contract. Even if the *licensee-salesperson* checks off the box, denoting *designated agent*, you are not agreeing even if you sign.

Agreeing takes place when an agent or *licensee* provides you with what is generally referred to as an *exclusive buyer agency agreement*.

• Don't confuse the *exclusive buyer agency agreement* with *true exclusive buyer agency*, the *practice/brokerage*.

True exclusive buyer agency is the practice of representing homebuyers only and never taking listings or representing sellers.

The accepted definition of *exclusive buyer agency*, brokerage, or representation has prevailed for the past twenty years or more supported by authors, two real estate industry's trade associations, and others.

The traditional real estate industry, however, uses the term *exclusive buyer agency agreement* as an apparent sales tactic and apparently as a way to confuse homebuyers into thinking a given firm will exclusively represent them even though the firm has made no such promise.

A listing contract with a seller is called an *exclusive right of sale agreement* and not an *exclusive seller agency agreement*, so it is easy to see the possible deception that the traditional real estate industry tries to pull over on unsuspecting homebuyers.

- What is in the *exclusive buyer agency agreement*, that you should watch out for?

Mainly, find the clause that states that if you are interested in a property listed by the *licensee* or another *licensee* in the company, you agree in advance to *dual agency* or *designated agency*.

A *True Loyal Agent*™ would never include such a clause in their agreement. If you sign a document containing the clause you give up your right to true agent loyalty and having someone watching your back.

If you sign such a document, you may no longer be protected and could find yourself pretty much on your own. In other words, *caveat emptor* − Buyer Beware.

Other concerns arise with traditional real estate industry homebuyer agreements, but such issues are beyond the scope of this book.

Remember that such agreements are legally enforceable contracts. Discuss them with an attorney before signing them.

They are generally used by traditional real estate companies to bind homebuyers to the company.

Even though a homebuyer may realize a mistake later and want out of the agreement, it will cost dearly. Getting out of a contract can be a financial trap, so be very careful.

- Don't see homes with multiple agents.

  Before leaving the subject of real estate *salespeople*, I must warn you of a hidden danger in making contact with more than one real estate *licensee*.

  Attending open houses, touring one or more homes with one or more *salespersons*, calling real estate *salespeople* for information about listings, or providing your name, email, and other contact information online can lead to your inability to find a true agent to represent you.

  It could also lead to you being liable for paying the compensation of two real estate agents.

  If you make contact with a real estate *salesperson* who supplies you with information about a property or who shows you a property that you later buy, the *salesperson* can make a claim to be paid a commission, even if you purchase the property through another agent or directly through the seller.

  Such a *salesperson* can make a claim for commission regardless of whether you actually met with or talked with the real estate *salesperson* or signed any documents with that *salesperson*.

You are free to use anyone you choose or no one at all to help you buy a home.

But if the home you buy was listed in a REALTOR®-operated Multiple Listing System (MLS), the agent can make a claim to be paid a commission on grounds that the agent introduced you to the property and thus is the *procuring cause of the sale.*

They do so through mandatory REALTOR® arbitration and thus potentially could take your current agent's commission away.

If that happens, you may end up liable for paying two commissions or at least making it very difficult for your current agent to keep their hard-earned commission.

It also means that some *True Loyal Agents™* won't want to take you on as a client if they think there might be a problem later getting paid.

What should you do to avoid such a problem?

Decide if you are going to use the services of a *True Loyal Agent™* to help you purchase a home.

As mentioned above, a *true exclusive buyer agent* or a *true single-party agent* is your best option.

If you are going to use such an agent, you absolutely should start doing so as early in the process as possible.

This will help you avoid the mistakes mentioned in this book and second this will prevent problems for a true buyer's agent in working for you.

Let the agent know if you have seen homes for sale or have been in contact with other agents, especially if you got information about a home you might be interested in.

There are steps the agent can take to avoid issues for them and for you, but they need to know that such a situation exists.

- Understand advertisements claiming that a so-called buyer agent works for free or at no cost. Of course, no agent works for free.

What the advertisement means is that the agent shares in commissions offered by the seller and the listing agent.

Multiple-listed property generally has a co-op fee offered to a buyer agent.

The co-op fee usually represents a percentage of the purchase price.

If the so-called buyer's agent claims to work for free or at no cost, it means the agent will accept a co-op fee as total compensation.

A buyer's agent will generally ask a buyer to sign a written exclusive right-to-represent agreement as discussed above that specifies compensation for the buyer agent.

The agreement will indicate the amount of the buyer agent's compensation, which often equals the co-op fee offered for the property.

I believe there is a problem with the buyer's agent agreeing to accept the offered co-op fee that is offered as the agent's total compensation.

You may not see all properties that may meet your needs.

Some listings offer a very low co-op fee to *buyer agents*.

As a result, many traditional real estate *licensee buyer agents* will review potential home listings to show buyers by seeing what the co-op fee is first.

If it isn't acceptable they throw that listing away even though it might be the most ideal property for the buyer

This practice has become more widespread with the advent of discount listing companies and listing agents who want to discourage other agents from showing their listings by not offering a reasonable co-op fee to *buyer agents*.

This is in order to increase their chances of selling the property themselves and collecting a double-dip commission.

A better way is for the buyer and the *buyer agent* to agree on a compensation method and an amount to be paid to the *buyer agent*.

It would also include an agreement as to how any differences between that amount and the co-op fee offered, plus any incentive bonuses offered, are to be handled.

For example, if the agreement called for the *buyer agent* to be paid 2.5% of purchase price and the co-op fee offered was 2% of purchase price the difference could be paid by the buyer at closing.

If the co-op fee offered was 3%, the *buyer agent* could rebate that difference to the buyer after closing.

That way there is no incentive for the *buyer agent* to show homes based on compensation offered by means of the co-op fee and/or incentive bonuses for a quick sale, for example.

One of the challenges that this system creates is the potential of ending up with the buyer owing additional money to the *buyer agent* at closing.

I certainly do not want to put a buyer client into a position of having to pay any part of my professional compensation out of pocket at closing.

So the goal is to treat any amounts owed as additional closing costs and work them into the purchase offer and negotiation strategy just as other closing costs are handled.

The potential amount that might be due is known before the offer is put together so it is fairly easy to take care of such a situation.

It is important for a buyer to find out upfront how an agent's compensation and any offered incentive bonuses will be handled.

Before signing an agreement, be certain it addresses such considerations.

- Is it a conflict if a *buyer's agent* is paid a percentage of purchase price? Not really.

Real estate agents are generally paid a success fee/commission as a percentage of purchase price.

However, you may perceive a conflict of interest when you have a *buyer agent* representing you whose job is to get yourself the lowest price.

The higher the purchase price you pay, the higher the commission to the *buyer agent*.

However, it really isn't a conflict of interest. Take a price difference of ten thousand dollars at a three percent commission—that equals three hundred dollars.

No professional *buyer agent* would encourage a buyer client to pay ten thousand dollars more for a property so that they could make three hundred dollars more themselves.

They know that they would benefit more by saving their buyer client ten thousand dollars so that the client would be happy with their service and refer them to others or use their services again in the future.

- Will the agent discount the fee? Don't be afraid to ask prospective agents if they discount or rebate part of their fee back to you or offer an alternative compensation model, such as a retainer and hourly fee instead of a percent of purchase price.

Keep in mind that agents I recommend working with are true fiduciary agents. They should receive higher compensation than a *salesperson* who isn't your true fiduciary agent.

If an agent is merely trying to sell you a home and in particular, trying to sell you a home that someone else in the agent's company has listed, you should ask for a rebate. After all, the agents are double-dipping the commission.

I have sometimes rebated part of my compensation.

As I mentioned above, I rebate bonuses or overages beyond whatever the agreed-upon compensation is between my buyer client and me.

A word about alternative compensation models: the contingency fee compensation model, being paid a percent of purchase price at closing, puts all the risk on the real estate *licensee*.

If a sale doesn't take place, the *licensee* doesn't receive compensation.

The retainer with an hourly-fee model puts the risk on the homebuyer.

In the hourly fee model, you, the homebuyer, pay a retainer fee upfront along with an hourly fee paid out of the retainer. Then at closing, you typically receive a refund of any co-op fee received by the agent along with any retainer fee left over after deducting all hourly fees.

The advantage for the agent is receiving compensation for the time expended regardless of whether or not you actually buy a home.

The advantage to the homebuyer is that, as long as you buy a home and don't spend a lot of the agent's time looking for the right home or putting together a transaction that closes, you may come out ahead.

The contingency fee model works best for homebuyers short of cash and who only have enough for the down payment, closing costs, and a contingency/reserve fund.

The retainer/hourly fee model works best for homebuyers who have the cash to pay a retainer and hourly fee along with a down payment, closing costs, and a contingency/reserve fund and who have a good idea of what they want so that their agent doesn't spend a long time putting a transaction together.

You should be able to find a *true exclusive buyer agent* or *true single-party agent* in Massachusetts by contacting MABA through the information provided above.

But if you can't and end up buying a home through a *licensee* with a traditional real estate company that takes listings, make sure that you try to find a smaller, perhaps single office company that doesn't have a lot of *licensees*.

As a result such an office may not have a lot of listings and hopefully none that you would be interested in.

As long as the office agrees to be your *buyer agent* and not a *designated* or *dual agent*, you should get decent true representation.

Make sure that any buyer agency agreement you sign doesn't include your agreeing in advance to *dual agency or designated agency* in the event you are interested in buying one of their listings. You should cross that section out.

Should that situation arise make sure they will refer you out to a *buyer agent* with another company just like a *true single-party agency* would and release you and the new agent you use from any liability for a commission.

For more information about *True Loyal Agent*s™ visit www.tomwemett.com/true-loyal-agent.

Chapter Six
Become Familiar with the Local Real Estate Market

It is vital that you know the market.

You must develop an intuitive feeling for value.

How do you do that? See lots of homes for sale.

You shouldn't buy the first home you see, although sometimes it ends up being the best of the bunch.

The only way to be sure about the home you decide to purchase is to get out and see other similar homes.

Also, only by seeing lots of homes will you know what to offer for the home you decide to buy.

Open Houses

Open houses are a great way to get a feel for available homes.

If your price range is up to $175,000, nevertheless tour homes up to $200,000. You may come across a home that compares to some you saw priced at $200,000 with an asking price of only $175,000.

Perhaps a motivated seller has priced their home to sell.

A word of caution: the real estate *salesperson* or seller holding an open house has a goal.

Each wants to find a buyer who falls in love with the home.

A *salesperson* or seller may ask you personal questions designed to help sell you the home.

You shouldn't give them personal information that could be used against you.

You shouldn't let them know

- how interested you are in the home

- how much of a mortgage you qualify for

- how much money you have for a down payment or where it comes from

- the price range of homes you are considering

- where you work

- or how much you make

To provide such answers is like playing poker with a mirror behind you that allows others to see your cards clearly.

Keep your cards close to your vest at all times but especially at an open house.

And please consider what you wear.

I had a client who was a doctor, and she always showed up wearing hospital garb with her stethoscope around her neck, thus telegraphing what she did and, in essence, her financial ability to buy. It made negotiating for a lower price a challenge.

And also watch what you are driving.

If you have a fancy car, leave it at home and take the family van.

I had another client who had won a substantial lottery. Real estate *salespeople* whom she worked with before working with me told sellers she had won the lottery.

She couldn't get a good deal no matter how hard she tried until she met with me.

I take the duty of confidentiality seriously. The seller of the home she bought had no idea where she got her money. That made it easier to negotiate a lower price.

If you have followed my advice as noted above and are already working with a *True Loyal Agent*™—an *exclusive buyer agent* or *true single-party agent*—make sure you have their business cards to give to the seller or the real estate *salesperson* holding the open house.

Tell the *salesperson* you have an agent and sign in with your name, but don't give them any contact information.

Take the *salesperson*'s business card and state that if you need further information or have questions about the home, you will have your agent contact the *salesperson*.

Doing so protects your *True Loyal Agent*™ from unscrupulous *licensees-salespeople* trying to use REALTOR® Arbitration to steal your loyal agent's compensation and eliminates annoying follow-up sales calls.

Seeing Homes with an Agent

Start seeing homes with the agent you have chosen.

Your agent will set up showings at your convenience to see homes that meet your needs.

If your agent shows you homes that don't meet your needs, ask why you aren't seeing homes more in line with what you want.

Perhaps there aren't any homes in the area that meet your requirements.

Then you must discuss what is available and whether or not you may have to wait to find something more appropriate or consider a higher price range or different location.

Staged Homes and Flips

When you tour homes in person, whether at an open house or with an agent, look for two things.

Has the home been staged or is the home being flipped?

Staging a home makes it look nice but may hide something such as water or pet stains temporarily covered with rugs on a hardwood floor.

The home also may look better with furniture placed by a designer/home staging professional than it will with your own furniture.

Try to imagine *your* furniture in the home and look beyond the staging to make sure the layout and condition of the home are satisfactory.

As for flipping, the market crash in 2008 brought out a lot of investors.

It is estimated that, following the crash, investors bought sixty-nine thousand homes nationwide with many still owned by investors.

Often such homes get cosmetic improvements but little else. They look great but often have hidden flaws.

If the home has been recently remodeled, look closely. Make sure the owner didn't put "lipstick on a pig," as the saying goes.

You should be suspicious of recent remodeling.

Your agent should be able to look up the sales history of the home to see when the seller bought it and at what purchase price.

You can then get an idea of improvements the seller made to the home to see if a price jump is justifiable.

If it appears the seller is trying to make a killing and really didn't do much, move on to another home.

Don't be a victim.

Layout and Traffic Pattern

The physical layout and traffic pattern of a home are also important.

Try to visualize living in the home.

Is it easy to carry groceries from the car to the kitchen? Perhaps the garage is on the opposite end of the home from the kitchen and requires bringing groceries through the living room or family room to get to the kitchen.

Think of other such uses of space to make sure a home is livable and meets your physical needs.

What about foreclosures, HomePath properties, bank-owned property (REO, Real Estate Owned), or HUD properties?

The problem for a first-time homebuyer for such properties is that they aren't for the faint of heart or inexperienced buyer.

Such properties are more for investors and experienced buyers.

The drawback involves that such properties are generally vacant and need a lot of work.

Utilities are off, and offers can't be made subject to home inspections.

Such homes are taken *as is*.

Many are hard to finance due to their condition, so standard financing is difficult to obtain.

My advice to most homebuyers is to stay clear of such properties.

You should stay focused on homes in nice condition and easily resold in from five to seven years should you decide to buy another home.

However, if it is your desire to pursue property in foreclosure or bank-owned, make sure the *buyer agent* you use is familiar with transactions for such a home and can be your guide to making a deal.

Such homes generally require special financing. Make sure you are pre-approved for such a mortgage.

Special loan programs allow borrowing money to buy the home as well as an amount to fix it up.

FHA 203K is one such mortgage program. I have helped some buyers go the FHA 203K route and understand it takes a lot of patience and time to accomplish such a purchase.

You must have a very cooperative seller and be willing to put up with a lot of paperwork and extended time for closing.

Chapter Seven
Look at All Available Homes

In most areas, agent listings are placed in a Multiple Listing System (MLS). MLS systems are usually operated by the local REALTOR® Association and all REALTOR® members have access to all listings by computer.

In Massachusetts, all MLS listings are available state-wide through the Multiple Listing System Property Information Network (MLSPIN).

However, some properties aren't listed and are known as for-sale-by-owner properties.

Make sure that, from the beginning, your agent shows you everything available within your specifications, including for-sale-by-owner properties if any are available in your area.

Be sure the agent shows you as many available homes as possible that appear best to meet your needs.

Many traditional agents' primary objective is to sell their own or their company's listings, and they may direct you to them before showing other listings.

They may not want to show you more than six or seven homes, and then they expect you to buy one.

They may steer you towards certain listings that offer them higher commissions and away from listings that offer a lower commission.

They probably won't show you for-sale-by-owner properties. They may be uncomfortable or aren't experienced working with for-sale-by-owner properties when representing a buyer.

In some areas, for-sale-by-owner properties aren't a high percentage of the market, but you should be on the lookout for them.

Make sure you consider enough homes and don't look only at three or four and pick one unless you find the perfect home at the right price.

Exclusive buyer agents and *true single-party agents*, *True Loyal Agents*™, will show you everything available that meets your needs, including for-sale-by-owner properties right from the very beginning.

If you are working with a traditional real estate sales agent, make sure the agent does the same.

Beware of the following tactic used by many traditional real estate industry *licensees-salespeople* to entice buyers to work with them.

They claim to have off-MLS listings, known as *pocket listings* or *coming soon listings* they can offer you exclusively at first.

Such promises are often empty.

A seller's best chance of selling for the highest price is to expose it to the entire market through the MLS.

What seller would want a real estate *salesperson* finding a buyer for their home before it is marketed?

The *salesperson* doesn't care about the seller or the buyer but rather simply focuses on making a deal and double-ending commissions.

Coming soon listings are often used in a hot sellers' market to create interest in advance of the home being available for viewing or to having offers presented.

It is used to create an auction atmosphere and a bidding war.

You may want to stay away from such homes. Ask what your agent thinks.

Your agent should also be willing to canvass homeowners in a neighborhood that you really like but where no homes are available that meet your needs or price range.

I canvassed several homeowners on behalf of a client who loved a particular condo-townhome project and wanted to live there.

We saw several for sale, but she wanted an end unit with a particular view.

I identified a dozen that would meet her needs and mailed out a letter to the owners indicating that I had a buyer client interested in their property if they were interested in selling.

I had three owners who responded saying they would sell.

I ended up putting a deal together on one at a very good price for my buyer client.

In my experience, *exclusive buyer agents* and *true single-party agents* seem to have more flexibility and desire than the traditional sales agent to find the right property for their buyer clients and seem to think outside of the box in order to help their buyer clients find and buy a suitable home.

Chapter Eight
Develop a Negotiating Strategy Before Making an Offer

In Massachusetts a two-step process is usually used for purchasing a home.

Initially there is an "offer to purchase" contract (known as the *contract to purchase real estate*) that lists most of the terms, conditions and contingencies that the buyer and seller agree to.

It acts like a memorandum of your final agreement, known as the *purchase and sales agreement (P&S)*.

The *contract to purchase real estate* is typically from two to seven pages long.

Any terms that are material to the transaction must be presented and agreed to in the initial *contract to purchase real estate* or they may not be included in the final *P&S*.

It is important to note that although the two-step process is prevalent throughout Massachusetts, the actual forms used and their names may be different.

I'm in north central Massachusetts, and here the custom is to use the MAR, Massachusetts' Association of REALTORS® forms which I'm referencing here.

These may differ from the forms used in the Boston area or North Shore or South Shore or Cape Cod areas.

Ask your agent or attorney which forms they use or prefer.

The names and content of the forms may differ but my comments still in general pertain to all the forms used.

The reason for the two-step process is probably so that the home inspections can be done and any negotiations with regard to repairs can take place and any such changes can be included on the *P&S*, which then is "cleaner" than it would be with offers and counter-offers.

By "cleaner" we mean that the final written agreement (the *P&S*) has no revisions or addenda changing the price or other terms of the contract.

Lenders must have a copy of the final signed *P&S* in order to process the loan and order the appraisal.

The appraiser will need to see a final contract, the *P&S*, in order to know what the final agreed-to purchase price is along with any other repair agreements between the seller and the buyer in order to do their appraisal.

Also, any negotiations for repairs that result in a reduction of price, a repair credit or agreement by the seller to complete repairs must be included in an addendum to the initial *contract to purchase real estate* in order to be included in the final *P&S*.

One of the clauses in the *contract to purchase real estate* is that the buyer and seller agree to sign a final *P&S* that is satisfactory to both parties by a certain date.

That date usually allows for enough time for the inspections to be done, repair negotiations (if any) and for the *P&S* to be written and the attorneys to review the final *P&S* before it is ready for signatures of the buyer and the seller.

Once a *P&S* is signed the initial *contract to purchase real estate* becomes void and whatever terms and conditions that were in it are no longer valid unless now in the *P&S*.

If a satisfactory *P&S* is not signed by the date stated in the *contract to purchase real estate*, then the signed *contract to purchase real estate* becomes the actual contract by which the transaction is completed.

Failure to agree to a *P&S* is not grounds for cancellation of the initial *contract to purchase real estate*.

This is a huge benefit for a buyer.

If it could be canceled by a seller just by not agreeing to sign the *P&S* then a seller could receive a higher offer while yours is in process, not agree to sign the *P&S* and then be free to sign the other deal.

As the *contract to purchase real estate* is drafted by your agent generally using a fill-in the blanks pre-printed form and not made subject to attorney approval, it is very important that you or your agent be in touch with your attorney to see what "material" items they recommend be included in the initial *contract to purchase real estate*.

I met with an attorney I recommend to my buyer clients, and she and I made a list of material items that I should include in the initial offer and attempt to negotiate for them to stay in the contract.

Most real estate *licensees* don't do this and the buyer's attorney is then bound to deal with whatever was in the initial contract and may not be able then to include material items that they feel should have been included initially.

Professional agents do know what items to add in the initial contract making the attorney's job a lot easier but also making sure that you are better protected.

Speaking of lawyers, just as I recommend working with a *True Loyal Agent*™, I recommend working with an experienced real estate lawyer.

Buying a home is one of the largest financial transactions that you are likely to make in your lifetime.

You should not make this major transaction without an experienced lawyer by your side to protect the multitude of complex issues involved in the process.

An experienced lawyer will take the confusion out of the transaction by taking time to explain the process while keeping you informed every step of the way.

A lawyer can give advice on all legal aspects of the real estate transaction.

A lawyer can handle every facet from the initial offer through the negotiation and execution of the *P&S* and finally through the transfer and recording of the deed.

Additionally, a lawyer can help you decide how to take title and assist with the consummation or closing process.

Buying a home should be a rewarding experience, not a painful one.

The right lawyer can make the conveyance as simple and as painless as possible for the client.

Knowing what to expect and being prepared at the closing can help eliminate stress and result in a pleasant experience.

Find a lawyer who understands how important this transaction is to you, and is committed to consistently providing a level of service that prepares you for this final step in your real estate transaction.

I interviewed several real estate lawyers in my area of Massachusetts and only recommend those aligned with my passion for providing true fiduciary services for homebuyers.

Your agent should have done the same thing that I have and the lawyer or lawyers they recommend should be fully attuned to operating as a team with your agent to secure the best outcome for you.

Price Considerations

- Find a starting point. Rules of thumb such as starting at ten percent off list price generally don't work.

  Some homes are overpriced by fifteen to twenty percent while others are priced on the money or maybe below market value.

In some tight markets, as we are experiencing in some areas of Massachusetts currently, paying above list price is often necessary due to a limited number of quality homes or condos for sale and a large number of buyers who want to buy a home or condo in those areas.

My advice: Regardless of the market situation, set the maximum price you would pay for the property.

Then start at a price below that maximum that is still supported by facts such as property condition and selling prices of other homes but that still allows for negotiation room with the seller.

And try to avoid a bidding war if that is what transpires at the time you are buying.

Some homes sell way above what they are worth.

Such a market isn't sustainable, and many buyers will regret overpaying for their homes.

Buyers overpaid from 2007 to 2009, and similar conditions are appearing currently during 2016-2017 in some areas of the country including in Massachusetts.

If, however, you are in competition with other buyers, you generally have one chance and must initially present your best offer.

- What did the seller pay for the property? If the seller recently bought the property and asks considerably more for it but did nothing to improve its value, it would be good to know so that you may be able to negotiate a better price, since the seller may have some cushion to work with.

- How long has the seller owned the property?

- Is the property being flipped?

- Was the property inherited?

- Does it appear the seller actually lived in the property?

  You may have decided to buy an investor-owned property. How well was the property maintained?

  Owner-occupants seem to take care of their property better than investors and their tenants.

- What improvements has the seller done since owning the property and what is the value of the improvements?

  To determine if there is some cushion in the seller's asking price that gives you better negotiating leverage if the seller has owned the property for a short time and is flipping it, you should have a sense of what they did to the property and what they may have invested.

- What are similar homes selling for in the area?

  Your agent should run a comparative market analysis (CMA) of similar homes sold and on the market.

You should know the market value of the house you want to purchase and whether it is in line or out of step with the asking price.

You should have hard evidence to support your offering price if lower than asking price in order for your offer to be credible.

Traditional real estate industry *salespeople* probably will show you the higher end of comparable homes to encourage a higher price.

Your agent should show you a wider range of sold homes so that you see that some homes sell well below the asking price for the home you are considering.

• What is the home worth *to you*?

Market data is one thing, but an intuitive feeling is another.

What other homes have sold for and the asking price of other homes on the market offer a guide, but what if the home is perfect for you or has features important to you?

The home may be worth more to you than to other buyers.

You should take such considerations into account in determining what the home is worth to you and what you are willing to pay for the home, even if it exceeds the market data valuation.

However, if like most homebuyers you will obtain a mortgage, the home must appraise for the purchase price or higher, or the mortgage will be based on the lower appraised amount and you would have to come up with more cash down payment to make up the difference.

- What defects or potential defects does the home have?

  You should make your offer subject to a home inspection and perhaps other inspections to make sure you aren't buying a money pit, which I discuss below.

- What maintenance has been deferred?

  I always look at the furnace to see if it has been serviced annually as it should be.

  If there is no service record on it and it looks like it hasn't been cleaned or serviced for several years or longer, I suspect the rest of the home hasn't been cared for.

  An unmaintained furnace should be a warning to assess other mechanical systems for problems.

- How is the neighborhood?

  Crime? Noise? Smells? Ease of access?

  You are the one who is going to live there.

  If you want to know how the neighborhood is, visit at different times of the day.

Call the local police department to ask about crime rates in the area.

Drive by with the windows down to see if there are any loud noises or obnoxious smells coming from an industry or farm close by.

Check on where the nearest airport is and what the flight paths are.

- Concerned about sex-offenders? Check out the website for the Sex Offender Registry Board (SORB): www.mass.gov/information-about-sex-offenders.

- What about low-balling?

  If the seller senses you are making a low-ball offer, the seller won't take your offer seriously and may not counter it.

  The seller may be put off by your actions and not later consider a reasonable offer from you.

When determining a negotiating strategy, it is also important to remember that price isn't everything.

You should also take into consideration your strengths and the strength of your offer.

- You should have as strong a *qualifying letter* from a lender as possible.

  Regardless, you will make your offer subject to obtaining financing on the terms you require, but provide the seller and the seller's agent with a *qualifying letter* that states that your credit, income, and assets have been reviewed and verified.

You also should determine how much of information on the *qualifying letter* you want to share with the seller and the seller's agent.

If you are qualified, for example, for up to a $250,000 purchase price and you are making an offer on a home with a $220,000 asking price, how do you present the *qualifying letter* to the seller and agent?

Do you black out the $250,000 figure and state that your qualification is sufficient for the price you are offering or do you show the actual qualifying purchase price?

Letting the seller and agent know what price you are qualified for may result in the seller countering at a higher price because the seller may believe that if you really want the home you can easily afford to pay more.

On the other hand, showing that you are qualified for more than what you are offering shows strength, and as long as you have predetermined the highest price you are willing to pay and stick to it, showing the qualified loan amount may work in your favor especially if you are competing with other offers.

Discuss the strategy with your agent to determine how the agent feels about it and what the agent recommends.

- Can you close quickly?

  If you are paying cash or are pre-approved for a mortgage and ready to close as soon as documents are ready to sign it is possible that a seller will give your offer greater consideration at a lower price if they have a strong need to close quickly and you are able to accommodate them.

- Can you delay closing?

  Perhaps the seller has a need to delay the closing. If they are building a new home they may need additional time before they are ready to move, in order to avoid a double move. If you can arrange for a longer mortgage commitment without it costing you anything and you have no problem with the extended timing of the closing this might work to your advantage in negotiating a lower price.

- Can you delay moving in after closing?

  Another option seller's sometimes would like is to stay in the home after closing for 30 to 45 days. They need the money from closing to buy their next home but perhaps would like some time in which to paint and improve the home they are buying before having to move.

  In such a case they enter into a written agreement approved by your attorney whereby they prepay you rent at closing for the time period you both agree to along with a security deposit to be held by your attorney in the event they don't move out when they are supposed to.

Consider the seller's motivation to sell.

- Is the home vacant or soon to be?

  The seller may be concerned about vandalism or carrying costs and willing to sell at a reduced price.

- Have the sellers purchased another home or do they have another home under contract subject to selling the home you want to buy?

  The seller may be carrying the costs of maintaining two homes. The seller may be very interested and motivated for a quick sale at a reduced price.

- Has the property been on the market for a long time as evidenced by expired listings with the current agent or previous agents?

  The seller may have been overly optimistic about their selling price. Perhaps the seller may be ready to deal.

- Are the owners divorcing?

  When walking through the home, look for signs of a separation or divorce. Does it appear that someone has moved out?

- Is the property in foreclosure?

  Often a property in foreclosure can be bought in a *short sale.*

If the market value of a home is less than what the owner owes on the mortgage, sometimes a lender will take less than the loan amount because doing so is preferable to foreclosing on a loan—hence the term *short sale*.

Beware, however, that although it makes financial sense for a lender to agree quickly to a *short sale*, sometimes a lender drags out a decision for months.

Generally, a *short sale* isn't the best route for a first time homebuyer.

However, if the home is in foreclosure and the seller has equity in the home, it is possible that the seller will consider a lower price rather than lose the home and equity later.

- Has a death or illness in the family forced a sale?

Often someone inheriting a home has no interest in owning it and wants it sold quickly to settle an estate.

Knowing about a death, illness, or inheritance can help with the negotiating process.

Other negotiating considerations include:

- What is the likely counter offer from the seller?

Try to envision different counters from the seller.

The seller can reject your offer, accept it, or counter it with changes, generally in the price.

What will be the amount of your next counter offer?

If you started at a price below what you feel the home is worth, you have room to move once you have an idea of the seller's potential flexibility.

- Should you ask for a closing cost credit, also referred to as a seller concession?

Many loan programs allow for a seller to help with a buyer's closing costs.

Seller concessions generally range between three and six percent of purchase price, depending on the requirements of the particular loan program.

However, the considerations are misnamed, as the seller really isn't providing a concession, as the name implies.

Rather the seller is providing a way for you to finance in some of your closing costs.

Say the seller is asking $200,000 but would take $190,000.

You would like the seller to help out with your closing costs and ask the seller to pay $8,000 as a closing cost credit and offer $190,000, with an understood net price to the seller of $182,000.

But the seller, wanting $190,000, counter-offers at $198,000, then paying $8,000 toward your closing costs and netting $190,000.

Who paid the $8,000? You probably did, because your price may have increased by $8,000 over what you may have paid for the home without the concession.

Use seller concessions for closing costs if necessary and keep them toward the lower end of what is allowed.

It may be better to get help from a relative whom you can pay back over two to three years then to increase the purchase price and mortgage to pay back with interest over from twenty to thirty years.

Also, some loan programs include a bank-provided closing cost credit.

Such programs generally, however, end up with a slightly higher interest rate to offset the cost of the credit.

Another factor to consider is that the home has to appraise at the higher price that includes the seller closing cost credit in order for you to obtain the full mortgage you are seeking.

- How do you handle repair issues?

  Should you ask the seller to make certain repairs, ask for a repair credit, or offer a lower price and handle repairs yourself?

  If you ask the seller to make repairs, will the repairs be done in a good workmanlike manner?

  The seller may independently complete repairs or get a neighbor to help out even though neither the seller nor the neighbor has adequate skills or experience to do repairs well.

I recommend getting a repair credit at closing or reducing the price so that the buyer makes repairs by hiring tradespeople suitable to the buyer.

A caveat concerns whether intended repairs are major or minor and whether the inspection requires them before closing.

If the lender's appraisal comes up with repairs or if the repairs will be major, the lender may not allow a repair credit, may require that repairs be made prior to closing, or may hold money in escrow pending repairs.

Sometimes, a buyer and seller can negotiate repair credits privately at closing, but often closing documentation must show details about repair credits, which can bring scrutiny by the lender about the extent of repairs that may be needed.

Discuss the matter of repair credits with your agent and your attorney.

- What can you give up in negotiating that isn't as important to you as may be to the seller?

Sometimes it makes sense to ask for things in your initial offer that aren't really important to you but that may be used later in negotiating as a give-back to the seller.

An example may be asking for the washer and dryer. Washers and dryers seem to be personal to some people.

So asking for the seller to include the washer and dryer and then having the seller ask for them back may be a good negotiation tool to get a better price.

Perhaps you have your own washer and dryer or want to buy new ones, so such a tactic may work well for you.

Successful negotiating is a complex process.

You should be aware of the nuances of negotiating in order to get the best price and terms.

A strength of a good buyer agent is the experience of negotiating on behalf of buyer clients every day.

Good buyer agents have developed knowledge and techniques to help their buyer clients consistently achieve success in the homebuying process.

Before you sign an initial contract to purchase real estate, do your homework.

Develop a strategy.

Seek assistance.

Don't be afraid to walk away if the seller refuses to meet your price and terms.

You may still be part of a consummated deal several months down the line at your price and terms if the seller softens up a bit and no other offers come in.

Be patient, and you may be rewarded with a great deal on a home.

One buyer client of mine made an offer once a month for four months on a home and finally had the fourth offer accepted at a lower price than their initial offer.

My client got a great deal on the home simply by waiting out the seller, a relocation company.

Chapter Nine
Include Contingencies for Property Inspections

You may want to have someone knowledgeable about building structural components and mechanical systems go through the home with you prior to writing a purchase offer.

By doing so, you will have information available to help in determining your negotiating strategy.

A person knowledgeable about buildings and mechanical systems could be a relative, a contractor, or your real estate agent.

Whomever you consult, get information in the form of personal opinions from such knowledgeable individuals without the expense of a formal inspection.

Make sure the person you rely on really is knowledgeable about property evaluation.

A word of caution: When soliciting the opinion of a real estate agent, keep in mind that a *dual agent* or *designated agent* also represents the seller and won't be looking out only for you as buyer.

Only rely on the opinion of an agent if that agent is acting as your agent and only if that agent has the experience, knowledge, and background to produce a valuable opinion.

By law, agents must disclose known defects.

Many agents don't investigate the condition of property they list because they would have to tell prospective buyers if they found problems.

In Massachusetts, sellers are not required to disclose known defects or provide you with a seller's property disclosure.

As a buyer, you should, however, ask for the seller to fill out and sign a *seller's statement of property condition*. Several forms for the purpose are used in Massachusetts.

You may encounter resistance to the request. It doesn't mean that the seller necessarily wants to hide something. It is more an issue of legal liability.

If the seller fails to disclose something or makes a mistake providing information, it increases the seller's legal liability to you.

Not providing the form removes potential liability.

A negotiating tool would be to ask for a *seller's statement of property condition* but then drop your request during negotiation to give you leverage toward getting something else more important to you.

Even if the seller provides such a disclosure, be cautioned that the form is not a substitute for property inspections.

Problems may exist in the home that the seller doesn't know about and/or doesn't list on the disclosure.

In Massachusetts, regardless of other considerations, a seller must deal with three property issues and disclosures.

- The first concerns lead paint if the home was built before 1978. Lead poisoning is the nation's number one environmental disease affecting children.

There are both a federal lead paint disclosure act and a more stringent Massachusetts Childhood Lead Poisoning Prevention Program (CLPPP) concerning lead paint.

Under both the federal and state requirements, a seller must disclose known instances of lead paint and provide copies of any testing results showing lead paint.

Both laws allow for a ten-day period for a buyer to conduct a lead-paint test at buyer's expense if the buyer desires.

More information about lead hazards in the home can be obtained from the US Environmental Protection Agency (EPA) at https://www.epa.gov/lead.

Find the EPA publication, *Protect your Family from Lead in Your Home*, at www.tomwemett.com/EPA-lead-booklet.

Under the Massachusetts Childhood Lead Poisoning Prevention Program, a seller of a home built before 1978 and the seller's real estate agent must provide a Property Transfer Lead Paint Notification package to any prospective buyer. The eleven-page document provides information to a prospective buyer about Massachusetts lead paint requirements. See www.tomwemett.com/MA-Lead-Paint-Notification.

The Massachusetts Lead Law applies only to homes built before 1978 where a child under six lives or will live. There is nothing in either the federal or state laws requiring a seller to delead or abate lead paint hazards. Of course, a seller may want to do that so that a buyer won't have to.

If a buyer has a child under the age of six living in the household or is expected to have such a situation take place in the future, the buyer should investigate the Massachusetts Lead Law in more detail and perhaps have lead paint testing done as part of the purchase process in order to assess the cost of deleading the home that meets the requirements of the lead law.

There is no requirement for a lead inspection or risk assessment before a sale, but having one done as part of purchase contingencies to determine the cost to bring the home into compliance later may make sense. Of course, a buyer could forego the process and deal with it after closing with the understanding that, if a child under the age of six will be residing in the home, the owner or eventual owner must have the home deleaded or brought under interim control within ninety days of taking title to comply with the lead law.

Interim control is defined as a set of temporary measures that property owners can take to correct urgent lead hazards especially peeling or chipping lead paint and lead dust. A licensed risk assessor does an initial risk assessment to determine the extent of necessary work to bring the home into compliance. The owner then has ninety days to provide proof of completed work and a Letter of Interim Control issued and signed by a licensed risk assessor. Such a letter is good for one year but can be renewed for one additional year with a new risk assessment. At the end of the two-year period, the owner is required to delead the home fully.

Fully deleading a home is defined as correcting the following lead hazards: peeling, chipping, or flaking lead paint, plaster, or putty; intact lead paint, other coating, or putty on movable parts of windows with sills five feet or less from the floor or ground and surfaces that come in contact with movable parts; intact lead paint or other coating on "accessible mouthable surfaces," which a young child could chew. Such surfaces include woodwork, such as doors, door jambs, stairs, stair rails, and window casings.

A Letter of Compliance must be issued and signed by a licensed lead inspector by the end of the two year term. The letter will say either that there are no lead paint hazards or that the home has been deleaded.

More information about the Massachusetts Childhood Lead Poisoning Prevention Program (CLPPP) can be found at: https://www.mass.gov/orgs/childhood-lead-poisoning-prevention-program

- The second requirement Massachusetts sellers must address concerns a private waste disposal system, also known as a septic system.

If the home is serviced by such a system, under Title Five of the Code of Massachusetts Regulations, an approved inspector must inspect the system for its compliance with the local board of health regulations within two years prior to the sale.

If the system isn't in compliance, the board of health will issue an order to repair or replace it.

The seller isn't required to pay for repair or replacement of the septic system, but the buyer probably won't be able to get a mortgage unless the septic system complies.

Buyers should insist that the seller pay for any required repair or replacement prior to closing and that the seller provide a certificate showing the system complies with *Title Five* at closing.

The matter of septic system approval should be included in the list of material items in the *contract to purchase real estate* if the home is serviced by a septic system and the seller hasn't already provided the buyer with a *Title Five certificate of compliance*.

Bringing a septic system up to today's code could cost thousands of dollars.

Make sure also that the system as certified is sufficient for the number of bedrooms that are actually in the home. If the certification says it is for three bedrooms and there are four bedrooms the system shouldn't pass.

- The third Massachusetts requirement for sellers to address is that the property must be inspected by the local fire department for compliance with the state's smoke alarm regulations prior to the property selling.

  The seller commonly arranges for the inspection and obtains the required compliance certificate as part of the seller's responsibility prior to closing.

Once the *contract to purchase real estate* is signed, it is prudent to pay for a professional property inspection.

Property inspectors are available in most areas.

The best ones to engage issue reports that meet or exceed internationally accepted standards of the American Society of Home Inspectors. Find reports and information at www.homeinspector.org/Why-Choose-an-ASHI-Inspector or the National Association of Certified Home Inspectors, www.nachi.org/blind.htm.

The extent of such a general inspection depends on the home you want to buy.

You also may want to consider engaging specialists for additional inspections and tests that may be applicable to the home you want to buy, including:

- Radon Testing – www.epa.gov/radon. From the EPA *Citizen's Guide to Radon: Radon is a cancer-causing, radioactive gas. You can't see radon. And you can't smell it or taste it. But it may be a problem in your home.*

  Radon is estimated to cause many thousands of deaths each year. That's because when you breathe air containing radon, you can get lung cancer. In fact, the Surgeon General has warned that radon is the second leading cause of lung cancer in the United States today. Only smoking causes more lung cancer deaths. If you smoke and your home has high radon levels, your risk of lung cancer is especially high.

  Radon can be found all over the U.S. Radon comes from the natural (radioactive) breakdown of uranium in soil, rock and water and gets into the air you breathe. Radon can get into any type of building—homes, offices, and schools—and result in a high indoor radon level. But you and your family are most likely to get your greatest exposure at home, where you spend most of your time.

  You should test for radon. Testing is the only way to know if you and your family are at risk from radon. EPA and the Surgeon General recommend testing all homes below the third floor for radon.

  You can fix a radon problem. Radon reduction systems work and they are not too costly. Some radon reduction systems can reduce radon levels in your home by up to 99%. Even very high levels can be reduced to acceptable levels.

- Lead Paint Testing – www.epa.gov/lead. From the EPA.gov website: *If your home was built before 1978, there is a good chance it has lead-based paint. In 1978, the federal government banned consumer uses of lead-containing paint, but some states banned it even earlier.*

  Lead from paint, including lead-contaminated dust, is one of the most common causes of lead poisoning. Lead paint is still present in millions of homes, sometimes under layers of newer paint. If the paint is in good shape, the lead paint is usually not a problem.

  Deteriorating lead-based paint (peeling, chipping, chalking, cracking, damaged, or damp) is a hazard and needs immediate attention. It may also be a hazard when found on surfaces that children can chew or that get a lot of wear-and-tear, such as: windows and window sills, doors and door frames, stairs, railings, banisters, and porches.

  Be sure to keep all paint in excellent shape and clean up dust frequently. Lead in household dust results from indoor sources such as deteriorating lead-based paint. Lead dust can also be tracked into the home from soil outside that is contaminated by deteriorated exterior lead-based paint.

  Renovation, repair or painting activities can create toxic lead dust when painted surfaces are disturbed or demolished. Learn more about hiring lead-safe certified contractors.

  At www.tomwemett.com/EPA-lead booklet, you can obtain a copy of the EPA booklet, *Protect Your Family from Lead in Your Home.*

- Mold Testing – www.epa.gov/mold. From the EPA's website: *Molds are usually not a problem indoors, unless mold spores land on a wet or damp spot and begin growing. Molds have the potential to cause health problems. Molds produce allergens (substances that can cause allergic reactions) and irritants. Inhaling or touching mold or mold spores may cause allergic reactions in sensitive individuals.*

  Allergic responses include hay fever-type symptoms, such as sneezing, runny nose, red eyes, and skin rash. Potential health effects and symptoms associated with mold exposures include allergic reactions, asthma and other respiratory complaints.

  There is no practical way to eliminate all mold and mold spores in the indoor environment; the way to control indoor mold growth is to control moisture. Fix the source of the water problem or leak to prevent mold growth.

  Reduce indoor humidity (to from thirty to sixty percent) to decrease mold growth by: venting bathrooms, dryers and other moisture-generating sources to the outside, using air conditioners and de-humidifiers, increasing ventilation, and using exhaust fans whenever cooking, dishwashing and cleaning.

- Chimney Cleaning and Inspection – www.csia.org. From The Chimney Safety Institute of America's website: *The primary job of a chimney service professional is to aid in the prevention of fires related to fireplaces, wood stoves, gas, oil and coal heating systems and the chimneys that serve them.*

Chimney sweeps install, clean and maintain systems, evaluate their performance, prescribe changes to improve their performance, and educate the consumer about their safe and efficient operation.

I'll add some observations.

I've seen high-efficiency furnaces installed that vent out the sidewall of the basement where only a hot water tank was left to vent out the original chimney.

Often the hot water tank can't draft properly through the large opening that was for both a furnace and a hot water tank.

In such situations either a high efficiency hot water tank should have been installed or a smaller chimney liner should have been installed for the hot water tank alone.

Such situations may be pointed out by a general home inspection leading to the need for the chimney inspection.

However, that would probably require an extension of the home inspection contingency.

I prefer to handle it simply by means of a chimney inspection at the same time as the general home inspection.

- Furnace Cleaning and Inspection—Forced air furnaces circulate air that has been heated in an oil, propane, gas or wood fired furnace by means of a "heat exchanger."

Older furnaces had heat exchangers made out of cast iron that were very thick but not very energy efficient.

Modern furnaces use a thinner, more efficient material that sometimes doesn't hold up.

In either case, cracks in the heat exchanger allow toxic gases to enter your living space and produce life-threatening situations.

For the home heated with a forced air furnace, place carbon monoxide detectors throughout to notify occupants if toxic gases are present, when those inside should immediately leave the home.

I recommend that, if the furnace hasn't been regularly serviced, the buyer arrange for an unbiased heating contractor to clean and inspect the furnace at the buyer's expense to make sure the furnace doesn't have small cracks that could lead to major cracks that would allow toxic gases to circulate throughout the living space.

The only way to check a heat exchanger is to pull the furnace apart and use a mirror to reach and inspect hidden areas.

If cracks are found, renegotiate your contract to get the heat exchanger replaced—sometimes under warranty—or get a credit towards a new furnace.

I have seen one-year-old furnaces with cracks developing in the heat exchanger.

So, regardless of the age of the furnace, consider having it cleaned and inspected as part of your inspection contingency.

- Wood-Damaging Pest (termite) Inspection—I recommend a termite inspection but also checking for other wood damaging insects such as carpenter bees and carpenter ants.

Usually one will see some evidence of insect pests such as saw dust or holes in fascia boards where woodpeckers have poked holes in the wood trying to get to ants or bees.

- Swimming Pool Inspection—If there is a swimming pool and you intend to use it, have a pool company inspect the pool if it is open and operating.

If it isn't open, ask when it was last opened and if it was closed by a pool company.

If it is out of season for pool use, you may have to take the pool as is and hope it works.

If it was properly closed the previous season, chances are it will be okay.

- Well Testing—If the property has a well, get the water tested for iron, mineral content, sulfur, and bacteria as well as flow and pressure.

Bacteria should be immediately addressed.

High iron content can stain plumbing fixtures and clothes.

High sulfur content can produce foul-tasting water and foul smells.

Water filtration systems are available to manage such issues, including removal of bacteria. Visit www.culligan.com/homes/solution-center for more information on water issues and solutions.

- Septic Inspection and Certification—The seller should obtain and pay for septic inspection and certification. Title Five of the Massachusetts Environmental Code requires septic system inspection and certification, as discussed above.

  Regulations require that septic systems and cesspools be inspected by a licensed inspector "at or within two years prior to the time of transfer of title."

It is important that the initial contract to purchase real estate contain a contingency clause stating that the offer is subject to whatever testing the prospective buyer desires and that testing results and inspections must be satisfactory to you or you may cancel the contract and have your deposit refunded.

Know the property you plan to purchase.

Have appropriate inspections and testing done as part of the deal.

Further negotiating may be in order in the event that testing and inspections indicate the need for a repair or replacement.

Making an offer contingent upon testing and inspections gives you leverage to re-negotiate with the seller, as you have the option to cancel the contract and receive a refund of your deposit if the seller does not make a repair or agree to a repair credit.

If your contract is canceled, it pressures the listing agent to consider problems with the home when attempting to sell it to future potential buyers: once a problem is found in the home, the law requires an agent to mention it to all future prospective buyers.

The seller may prefer to work out a deal with you rather than go through the whole process with another buyer.

In a hot market area, expect competing buyers to be encouraged by their traditional real estate *salesperson* to make their offers attractive by skipping the inspection contingency.

You shouldn't take on the risk of unknown problems with the home that you're stuck with after closing.

Play it safe. Include the inspection contingency.

If the seller accepts another offer, move on to another home.

You may have just avoided a money pit.

Chapter Ten

Know What Other Contingencies to Include in Your Offer

An offer to purchase or *contract to purchase real estate* written from the buyer's perspective should have numerous contingencies in it to protect the buyer, as previously noted.

The *P&S* will carry over contingencies from the initial *contract to purchase real estate* as well as additional legal conditions.

The attorney to whom I refer my buyer clients recommended certain contingencies I mention below.

Although the contingencies appear standard, some may not be appropriate for the area of Massachusetts where you want to buy.

Consult with your agent and your attorney to see which contingencies apply to your area.

Perhaps add others pertinent to the area where you want to buy.

Depending on the buyer's circumstances, the *contract to purchase real estate* and the *P&S* should be subject to:

Buyer Attorney's Involvement and Review

A real estate *licensee*'s duties are restricted to real estate.

Buying a home involves a lot of legal issues and thus requires the services of a knowledgeable real estate lawyer.

Consult with a real estate lawyer in advance about items and contingencies the lawyer considers material that should be included in the *P&S*, thus allowing your agent to include them in the *contract to purchase real estate* so that they will carry over to the final *P&S*.

Engineer/Property Inspection

See the above discussion. It is prudent to have a professional home inspection.

Other Structural and Mechanical System Inspections

See the above discussion. Professional home inspections are general in nature, and additional testing may be applicable.

Obtaining Financing and Mortgage Commitment

Even though you should have gotten a *bank qualifying letter*, the initial *contract to purchase real estate* and thus the final *P&S* must be worded to indicate that it is subject to obtaining required financing.

What if the interest rate rises sharply so that you no longer qualify?

You need a way to get out of the contract legally if your financing falls through so that you can get your contract deposit back.

Bank Appraisal Equal To or Greater than Purchase Price

In a tight market with many homes selling for asking price or more, it is important that the bank appraisal be equal to or greater than the purchase price.

The mortgage you get is based on the lower of the purchase price or the appraised value.

If the home appraises for less than the purchase price, you will be required to pay the difference in cash, which you may not have.

By including a contingency about the bank appraisal, you can renegotiate the price or cancel the transaction and get your deposit back.

Receipt and Approval of a Completed Seller's Statement of Property Condition

See the above discussion. If possible, get the seller to fill one out or work with the disclosure as a negotiation technique.

Sale of a Property Owned by the Buyer or Pre-Closing Possession by the Buyer, If Applicable

Sometimes a buyer's position involves having a home to sell or perhaps an expiring lease.

If the seller's home is vacant, perhaps you can to move into the home before it closes and you own it.

Consider special provisions for such situations and include them in the initial *contract to purchase real estate* in order for them to appear in the *P&S*.

Subject to Receipt of a Comprehensive Loss Underwriting Exchange (CLUE) Report

Make your offer subject to the seller obtaining and providing a CLUE report.

What is CLUE report? CLUE is a claims-information report generated by LexisNexis®, a consumer-reporting agency.

The report usually contains up to seven years of personal-property claims history.

Insurance companies report claims which they approve and pay out money, set up a file, or formally deny.

How do insurance companies use CLUE reports?

An insurer may request a CLUE report when you apply for coverage or request a quote.

The company uses your claims history or the history of claims at a specific property to decide if the company will offer you coverage and at what premium.

Insurance company studies show a relationship between past claims and claims you report in the future.

A buyer can't get the report directly for the prospective home and must request that the seller provide it. The Fair Credit Reporting Act entitles an owner to a free annual copy of the CLUE report. To request a copy, the owner must contact LexisNexis, Consumer Center, 866-312-8076, or online at: https://personalreports.lexisnexis.com/homesellers_disclosure_report/agent.jsp.

You should ask for the report for two reasons.

First, you want to see if any past claims will have an impact on your ability to get insurance and the price you will end up paying.

Second, you want to see if there were claims you should review with your home inspector so that he or she can look at the specific area(s) of the home where damage took place.

Such claims could be for fire damage, water damage, wind damage, or other physical matter that you should know about.

Subject to the Signing of a Truth in Lending in Real Estate (TRID) Rider

A TRID Rider is a **T**ILA-**R**ESPA **I**ntegrated **D**isclosure, now part of any real estate closing.

TILA stands for Truth in Lending Act. RESPA stands for Real Estate Settlement Procedures Act.

Sometimes delays occur when the requirements of TRID rules and regulations have not been met in a timely manner. The rider provides for extension of time periods in order to meet TRID requirements.

Closing Cost (Seller Concession) Credits

See the above discussion.

Include any request for a seller credit for closing costs in the initial *contract to purchase real estate.*

Subject to the *P&S* Being Mutually Satisfactory

The terminology "mutually satisfactory" may not appear in the *contract to purchase real estate* form typically used in your area, so it may be necessary to add it.

Ask your agent and attorney if the terminology should be included in your area of Massachusetts.

Title Five Inspection Report

See the above discussion.

If the property is serviced by a septic system or cesspool, you should include a clause in the *contract to purchase real estate* making your offer subject to the seller providing at seller's expense a Title Five inspection report showing that the septic complies with Title Five of the Massachusetts Environmental Code.

If one can't be provided due to the season some provision should be made to ensure it is inspected and is in compliance.

Title Five allows for an inspection to take place within six months after a transfer/closing if weather conditions preclude an inspection at the time of transfer.

Banks usually won't lend money on a home with a septic system unless it has a Title Five Inspection report showing that the system complies.

If the seller doesn't have a report showing the system complies, your attorney may have to work with the bank and the seller's attorney about an escrow agreement so that money is available to bring a system into compliance and the buyer doesn't end up having to take care of it later out of pocket.

Chapter Eleven
Continue to Monitor and Follow Up

The closing date indicated in a purchase and sale contract is a *target date*.

Too many buyers and sellers assume that the closing will take place on the projected date.

However, very rarely does it happen unless someone monitors and follows up with the transaction.

Someone must make sure:

- that the appraisal gets done on time
- that the appraised value of the home at least equals the purchase price and, if not, you and the seller should renegotiate the price down to the appraised amount or if you do not wish to continue, the contract can be canceled
- that the appraiser and lender require no repairs or further repairs
- that you and the seller agree who will do which repairs and who will pay for repairs if repairs should be made before closing
- that repairs get done and are re-inspected in timely manner
- that a written mortgage commitment gets issued on time

- that contingencies of the mortgage commitment are taken care of

- that the seller's attorney has located the abstract of title, sent it for re-dating if that applies for your area, and ordered the survey, if that applies for your area

- that your attorney has reviewed title documents and the proposed deed and approved of them or asked the seller's attorney to revise the title document so you get unchallengeable ownership of the property

- that a prospective closing time and date are scheduled

- that the closing documents will be delivered on time and that you will receive the *closing disclosure* within three business days before the closing date

Sound confusing and time consuming? You bet. And nearly every step must be monitored in order to have a closing on or near the anticipated, contracted closing date.

Lots of disappointments result because no one monitored the process.

Most buyers don't know what is involved in closing on a house purchase, and therefore buyers should not be expected to monitor the process.

Of course if no one coordinates the process, the buyer will have to or face not closing on time.

It isn't good enough to contact your attorney or your lender and have your attorney or lender say everything is under control and not to worry.

Be sure you have a single professional keeping track of the process.

Your real estate agent should do it. Ask him or her what services are provided once your *P&S* is signed and whether the agent will actively stay on top of things.

I think of myself as the orchestra conductor. I know everyone's role and when they should perform. I keep the process humming along smoothly and under control.

Make sure that your agent agrees in advance to monitor the closing process. Otherwise you may be greatly disappointed.

Title Insurance

A quick word about title insurance. A mortgage company will require a *lender's* title insurance policy covering it as lender to protect its interest in the event a concern comes up later that clouds title to the property.

Most title matters are resolvable but require lawyer involvement. The lender's title insurance pays for the lawyer and other legal costs to clear the title.

In an extreme situation, when a title can't be cleared and the property can't be sold, the title insurance company will reimburse the bank for the amount of the mortgage, but you will lose any equity you may have in the property.

At closing, your attorney should offer you an *owner's* or *fee title insurance* policy that protects your equity in the property.

It is a one-time fee due at closing to protect you from previously undiscovered title defects during ownership as well as after you sell, should a title problem become apparent after you have sold and moved.

Most lawyers recommend it, and I do, too. Your attorney can explain it more fully and provide an estimate of the cost.

It would be wise to discuss the pros and cons of obtaining title insurance with your attorney prior to closing to make the closing go as smoothly as possible.

Title Wording

Another thing to discuss with your attorney prior to closing is how to take title of the property. For two or more buyers or a married couple, there are several available options that you should understand.

Co-owners in Massachusetts who buy real estate have three choices as to how to hold title in the deed:

- as tenants in common
- as joint tenants
- as tenants by the entirety (available only to married couples)

Ask your attorney to explain the differences to you and help you decide on your best option.

Chapter Twelve
Prepare for and Foresee
Problems at Closing Time

There is much yet to be done once the closing date is set.

Homeowner's Insurance

Usually the buyer must obtain an insurance binder, pay a full year's insurance premium in advance, get a receipt for the payment, and have copies faxed to the buyer's attorney before a closing can be set.

Start shopping early for homeowner's insurance, and don't wait until you have a mortgage commitment.

You will have to provide the insurance company with a *mortgagee clause* found in your mortgage commitment, but in the meantime, start the shopping process.

Often you can get a discount if you have your car and home insurance with the same company.

But there is a possibility that you will have difficulty obtaining insurance on a home that has had numerous claims by previous owners.

Better to determine if there will be a problem early enough to ensure you can get a reasonably priced policy.

Your insurance agent may be able to obtain the CLUE report if the seller isn't willing to provide it to you, because insurers generally use it to rate insurance policies.

Utilities

The buyer should call utility companies to transfer service into the buyer's name to include phone, cable, internet, and gas, electric, refuse collection, water, propane or fuel oil deliveries, as applicable.

Final Inspection

Next comes the final walk-through inspection.

The inspection takes place shortly before closing as the final opportunity for the buyer to see the home they are buying.

Use the final walk-through inspection

- to make sure that the home remained in the condition it was when you entered into the contract to buy it
- to check for water leaks, damage from movers, yard damage from storms or other events, or other adverse changes
- to make sure personal property such as appliances or window treatments included in the sale remain in place
- to check for instruction booklets for appliances and mechanical systems
- to make sure remote garage door openers remain
- to assure that a set of keys will be at closing for you, and
- to ascertain that utility meters have been read and meter reads called in or the fuel oil tank or propane

tank levels checked for reimbursement back to the seller for fuel left in the tank

Review of the Closing Disclosure

Once all contingencies in the contract have been cleared, all paperwork and title searches completed you are ready to proceed with a closing where you exchange money for a deed to the home.

Part of the closing process involves a review of a preliminary closing statement known as the *closing disclosure*. At closing, the *loan estimate* discussed in Chapter Three must closely match the final figures on the *closing disclosure*.

That is done to make sure that items don't appear on the *closing disclosure* that didn't appear on the *loan estimate*.

It also allows you time to review the individual items with your mortgage source in the event there are discrepancies.

The Closing Disclosure Explainer, available online at www.consumerfinance.gov/owning-a-home/closing-disclosure, should be used to double-check that all the details about your loan are correct on your *closing disclosure*.

Lenders are required to provide your *closing disclosure* three business days before your scheduled closing.

Use the days wisely to resolve problems. If something looks different from what you expected, ask why.

Actual costs at closing should be very close to the estimates. Often, differences are accidental, and you have time to get them corrected before closing.

Trying to get a bank to refund money after the fact or attempting to get things changed at closing will be a frustrating process.

If changes must be made on the *closing disclosure*, the closing will have to be postponed while a new *closing disclosure* is prepared and a new three-day time period takes place between your receipt of the revised *closing disclosure* and closing.

Preparation for the Closing
Know What Items to Bring to Closing, Including

- a cashier's check payable according to your attorney's instructions for the total amount you must pay

- your driver's licenses or other photo identification so the lender can verify your identity

- the original insurance binder and paid receipt, even if not required and

- perhaps your mortgage commitment and lender *loan estimate* for reference

Scam Warning: You may receive an email or letter directing you to send money for the closing to a closing agent.

Verify requests for deposits directly with your agent and/or attorney to make sure that such requests are legitimate.

The Actual Closing

If someone has diligently monitored the process, has helped you prepare for the closing, and has reviewed the *closing disclosure* with you, the closing should be a breeze.

Many times, however, sufficient preparation isn't done in advance of closing. Some matters often get left to be settled at closing.

And closings often become battlegrounds.

It helps to have a professional, knowledgeable agent working only for you at the closing to make sure that all goes well.

With preparation, the right agent, and right attorney, enjoyable closings may take less than an hour.

Real estate closings may take place at the lender's attorney's offices, your attorney's office, the lender's office or sometimes at a real estate office, usually wherever it is most convenient for all parties.

Sellers can sign papers in advance, and some do. Others come to the closing.

The buyer has to come to a closing in order to sign the mortgage and other documents.

The buyer should be accompanied by the buyer's attorney and should be accompanied by the buyer's real estate agent.

Professional buyer's agents do attend closings, monitor the process leading up to the closing, and in general do whatever must be done to ensure a smooth transaction.

Make sure you get copies of all signed documents from the closing, including temporary payment coupons for your mortgage payment.

If the lender fails to get your payment coupon book sent to you on time, you are nevertheless required to make payments when due.

Coupons may be given to you to make that easier for you in the event there is a delay getting the official coupon book to you.

At closing, you probably will be offered an opportunity to sign up for automatic withdrawal of funds from your checking or savings account to pay the mortgage each month.

It is wise not to sign up at the time of the closing but rather later after you have made several payments to make sure all documentation is accurate.

You can sign up for automatic payments at any time, so wait a month or two before you decide to do that.

Also wait to set up bi-weekly mortgage payments if applicable.

Wait a month or two and then contact the lender to make arrangements if you want.

After the Closing

You can celebrate. You did it.

You own your own home. Congratulations.

But wait. There are still some things you need to do now that you have closed.

- You should immediately go to your new home to make sure everything is okay and hasn't changed since your walk-through inspection before closing.

  If anything material has changed, contact your attorney and your agent immediately.

  Your attorney may be able to put the recording of the deed on hold while the concern gets worked out, thus pressuring the seller to make things right or risk not receiving sale proceeds.

- Make sure you do a change of address with the USPS.

  Go to: www.usps.gov and click on *Get Started* under the section *Making a Move?* to make the changes online. It will cost you a dollar charged to a credit card to verify your identity.

  You can also go to a local postal service office and ask for the USPS moving kit. You also need to contact credit card companies and other vendors you do business with to provide them with a new address.

- You should also as soon as possible re-key all locks in the home.

  You have no way of knowing who has keys to the property. Until you re-key locks, you are vulnerable to someone using a key to gain unsanctioned access to your home.

- You should also check on the utilities to make sure they are in your name and that meters were properly read.

  If you didn't arrange with the utility companies in time to transfer utilities into your name, chances are the seller canceled them and you may find them inactive.

  If that happens, you may experience a challenge in reactivating utility service. Make sure you cancel the utilities at your former residence.

My sincere wish is that your homebuying adventure is in fact enjoyable and successful and without the drama that sometimes takes place during the homebuying process.

And most of all, my hope is that you don't get sold a home but instead end up buying the right home at the right price.

After all a home purchase is probably the biggest financial investment you will ever make. Follow your gut. Try to keep emotions out of the equation.

Surround yourself with professionals who care and are committed to being true fiduciaries, agents protecting you and looking out for your best interest at all times and in every situation and your homebuying adventure will be most enjoyable and successful.

If you have any questions about any of the subjects in this book or about buying a home in Massachusetts call me at 978-633-9090 or visit www.tomwemett.com for more homebuying information.

Online Resources for Massachusetts Homebuyers Beware!

The following summary of websites and URLs mentioned in the book groups them by subject matter to make it easier for you to access them. These are also available online at www.tomwemett.com/online-resources as hot clickable links directly to the websites and updated regularly to keep them current.

Credit and Credit Scoring

To obtain FREE credit reports from all three major credit bureaus: A federal law, the Fair and Accurate Credit Transactions Act of 2003—the FACT Act, requires that credit reporting agencies must provide one free credit report every twelve months.

The official web site is www.annualcreditreport.com.

For more information about credit reporting and credit scores: Go to www.myfico.com/credit-education/credit-report-credit-score-articles/.

You can also obtain all three credit reports and FICO scores for a one-time fee of about sixty dollars by going to: www.myfico.com/products/three-bureau-credit-report/

For additional information about credit reports: Go to the Federal Trade Commission's web site – www.ftc.gov.

Click on the *Get Your Free Credit Report* button on the right side.

The three major credit bureaus and their contact information are:

EQUIFAX—www.equifax.com 800-685-1111

EXPERIAN—www.experian.com 888-397-3742

TRANSUNION—www.transunion.com 800-888-4213

Information about credit repair scams can be found at: www.consumerfinance.gov/ask-CFPB/how-can-I-tell-a-credit-repair-scam-from-a-reputable-credit-counselor-en-1343/

Mortgages

The Consumer Financial Protection Bureau (CFPB), is an excellent source of information about mortgage financing and homebuying. Go to the agency's website at www.consumerfinance.gov and check under *Consumer Tools* for more information about a number of financial related subjects, including *Owning a Home.*

CFPB has information in the *Know Before You Owe* section about two new forms, *Loan Estimate* and *Closing Disclosure* at www.consumerfinance.gov/know-before-you-owe.

Find more information about the *Loan Estimate* at www.consumerfinance.gov/owning-a-home/loan-estimate.

More information about the *Closing Disclosure* is available online at www.consumerfinance.gov/owning-a-home/closing-disclosure.

Massachusetts hosts special mortgage programs. See One Mortgage, www.mhp.net/one-mortgage/why-one. Other special loan programs are available through MassHousing, www.masshousing.com.

Homebuyers in Massachusetts will find down-payment and closing-cost-assistance programs and grants by going online to: www.tomwemett.com/down-payment-resource. This website links to an organization that maintains a database of down payment assistance programs throughout the country, including Massachusetts. The site allows you to input information to see if you qualify for any listed programs and grants.

Neighborhood and School Information:

Check out www.walkscore.com to see how an address rates in terms of proximity to shopping and entertainment.

Concerned about sex-offenders? Find information at www.mass.gov/information-about-sex-offenders.

For information about Massachusetts schools, check out www.greatschools.org/schools/cities/Massachusetts/MA/

Find a True Loyal Agent™

I've coined the name *True Loyal Agent*™ to refer to a real estate *licensee*/true agent who is with a company that represents real estate consumers as a true agent and never practices *dual agency or designated agency*.

For more information about *True Loyal Agents*™ visit: www.tomwemett.com/true-loyal-agent.

Find true professional *buyer agents* in Massachusetts by contacting MABA, the Massachusetts Association of Buyer

Agents, at 800-935-6222 or online at
www.massbuyeragents.org.

All **MABA** members are either *true exclusive buyer agents* or *true single-party agents* and thus are *True Loyal Agents*™.

A copy of the Massachusetts Mandatory Real Estate Licensee-Consumer Relationship Disclosure can be found here www.tomwemett.com/disclosure.

Homes For Sale

Investigate possibilities for Massachusetts *homes for sale* at www.tomwemett.com/mass-homes-for-sale. This link will take you to the Massachusetts MLS Property Information Network (**MLSPIN**) for access to listings statewide.

Go to www.realtor.com for the best up-to-date comprehensive database of listed property anywhere else in the country.

WARNING: Do not give out your email address, phone number, or other contact information. To do so will invite aggressive sales tactics by traditional real estate industry *licensees-salespeople*.

Home Inspection Information

The best home inspectors to engage issue reports that meet or exceed internationally accepted standards of the respected American Society of Home Inspectors, www.homeinspector.org/Why-Choose-an-ASHI-Inspector or the National Association of Certified Home Inspectors, www.nachi.org/blind.htm.

Radon Testing – www.epa.gov/radon.

Lead Paint Testing – www.epa.gov/lead.

For a copy of the EPA booklet, Protect Your Family from Lead in Your Home, you can download a copy at www.tomwemett.com/EPA-lead-booklet.

For a copy of Massachusetts Lead Paint Notification package: www.tomwemett.com/MA-Lead-Paint-Notification

For information about the MA Childhood Lead Poisoning Prevention Program (CLPPP): https://www.mass.gov/orgs/childhood-lead-poisoning -prevention-program

Mold Testing – www.epa.gov/mold.

Chimney Cleaning and Inspection – www.csia.org.

Water Testing and Filtration Systems www.culligan.com/home/solution-center

Other Useful Links

CLUE Reports: More homebuyers are requiring home sellers to provide a CLUE, Comprehensive Loss Underwriting Exchange report as a contingency to a purchase offer. This Seller's Disclosure Report provides a five-year insurance loss history for a given address, without divulging personal and private information about a property owner. If the report for the property indicates that the property hasn't sustained an insurance loss within the past five years, a buyer can feel comfortable that insurance loss history of the property should not impact the availability or pricing of homeowners insurance. The

Fair Credit Reporting Act entitles an owner to a free annual copy of the CLUE.

To request a copy of the CLUE Seller's Disclosure Report, the owner must contact LexisNexis, Consumer Center, 866-312-8076, or online at: https://personalreports. lexisnexis.com/homesellers_disclosure_report/agent.jsp

Make sure you do a change of address with the USPS after you close on your home. Go to: www.usps.gov to make the changes online. Click on *Get Started* under the section *Making a Move?*

I firmly believe in and am passionate about true representation of real estate buyers and sellers and not the deeply ingrained sales culture that is so prevalent in the traditional real estate industry today. As such I have dedicated my real estate career to supporting true fiduciary representation whenever I can.

If you have any questions about any of the subjects in this book, Massachusetts Homebuyers Beware, or about buying a home in Massachusetts please call me at 978-633-9090 or visit www.tomwemett.com for more homebuying information.

Some Final Words

Thank you for your interest and for taking the time to read *Massachusetts Homebuyers Beware! The Cards are Stacked Against You*. Although it was written specifically for homebuyers, there are others who may have read it or are reading it as well. This section is for you.

For Traditional Real Estate Industry Licensees-Salespeople

If you are a traditional real estate industry *licensee-salesperson* or individual thinking about becoming a real estate sales agent with a company that practices *dual agency* or *designated agency*, I hope you consider joining the ranks of true real estate consumer protectors in Massachusetts.

I would like to hear from you and help you understand how you can stop being a typical real estate *salesperson* and start being a true consumer advocate for buyers and/or sellers as a *True Loyal Agent*™.

You will either learn much from this book or take offense at what I have written and discussed here.

Most real estate *licensees-salespeople* are ethical, professional, and hard-working.

It is the industry that troubles me.

I take issue with the deeply ingrained sales culture of pushing in-house sales and ignoring true common law principles of fiduciary representation of clients.

Disclosed *dual agency* is at least transparent. The buyer and seller must understand what they are giving up (Obedience to Lawful Instruction, Undivided Loyalty, and Full Disclosure of all Material Facts) and must give their informed consent.

Designated agency, on the other hand, is deceptive, misleading, and a fantasy.

Real estate consumers are led to believe that the conflict of interest resulting from trying to represent a homebuyer and a homeseller in the same transaction in the same company goes away simply by calling it something else.

Centuries of well-settled and established common law dictates that *no person can serve two masters.*

The industry's trade association promoted true representation of clients thirty years ago. From the National Association of REALTORS© (NAR), 1986 Publication, *Who Is My Client? A REALTOR'S® Guide to Compliance with the Law of Agency*:

The legal concept of agency with which this booklet is concerned is, however, beyond question the most fundamental of all the legal concepts applicable to the real estate profession and professional. It is the very nature and function of the real estate broker, appraiser and manager to be an agent. The law of agency literally defines the species and gives real estate practitioners their identity.

However, with large real estate companies relying more and more on an in-house sale revenue stream, true representation has taken a back seat.

If you agree, here is your opportunity to join a group of professionals who put true representation of clients ahead of the typical industry profit motive.

There are true fiduciary real estate companies operating throughout Massachusetts who would welcome an opportunity to discuss with you joining their companies.

Feel free to contact me at 978-633-9090 or through www.tomwemett.com to discuss in confidence. Visit: www.tomwemett.com/true-loyal-agent to find out more about being a *True Loyal Agent™*.

For Traditional Real Estate Broker-Owners or Broker Associates Who Would Like to Start a Brokerage

You do not have to operate as a *dual* or *designated agency*.

If you are a small firm with fewer than five full-time *licensees*, in-house transactions probably aren't a large revenue source for you.

Instead of downgrading your relationship with the consumer to *dual agency* or *designated agency* for the occasional in-house transaction, set yourself apart and gain a competitive advantage by providing true fiduciary, true agent duties at all times and in every situation to your buyers and/or sellers as a *true single party agency* or *exclusive buyer agency* or *exclusive seller agency*.

You can represent buyers and sellers—just not in the same transaction.

You refer your buyer or seller out to another true fiduciary agent with another company so that each receives true representation when there is the potential for an in-house transaction.

As an *exclusive buyer agent*, I refer potential seller prospects to listing agents all the time as I have chosen not to represent sellers.

There are dozens of true fiduciary agents like me throughout Massachusetts who would love to work with your referrals as well as send referrals your way.

The Massachusetts Association of Buyer Agents, MABA, as noted in this book, can help—www.massbuyeragents.org or 800-935-6222.

MABA has *exclusive buyer agency* members but also supports *single party agencies* that represent buyers and sellers but never in the same transaction and thus never as *dual agents* or *designated agents*.

Or contact me at 978-633-9090 or through www.tomwemett.com to discuss options or to find out more about being a *True Loyal Agent™*, visit www.tomwemett.com/true-loyal-agent.

As long as you have an interest in providing true fiduciary duties and services to real estate consumers in Massachusetts there are people including me who will help you get started and mentor you.

For Mortgage Lenders and Mortgage Originators

You should keep in mind that homebuyers place their trust and faith in you to find them the right mortgage and to guide them through the financing part of the homebuying process.

It is far superior for your customer or member to buy a home while working with the services of a true fiduciary agent who guarantees to protect your customer or member throughout the entire homebuying process rather than having them sold a home through a real estate *salesperson*.

You should understand who the right agent is, how to identify such an agent, and how to find one so that you can direct your customer or member to a *True Loyal Agent™*, as discussed in this book.

It makes sense for lending institutions to have a true fiduciary agent on the side of customers or members as a safeguard so that homebuyers do not overpay for a home, buy the wrong home, or buy a money pit.

This small group of real estate *licensees* is comprised of dedicated professionals to the idea of true representation rather than the deep-seated sales culture that is so prevalent in the traditional real estate industry today.

They and your customers and members deserve your support.

Refer your customers and members to MABA, the Massachusetts Association of Buyer Agents, at www.massbuyeragents.org or have them call 800-935-6222 to find a dedicated *True Loyal Agent™*.

For Real Estate Lawyers

You understand fiduciary agency and true agency.

Do you really believe that it is best for homebuyers to buy a home using the services of a *dual agent* or *designated agent*?

Your law firm has policies about conflict of interest and systems in place so that you rarely, if ever, end up representing two clients against one another. If there is a conflict, you refer one party out to another lawyer with another law firm.

Do you really believe that *designated agency* provides the same protections as true fiduciary agency for a homebuyer or homeseller?

Can you imagine such a situation in the legal profession? Can you imagine that your managing partner would designate one lawyer in the firm to work for one party and another lawyer in the firm to work for the opposing party?

It doesn't work for law firms, and it doesn't work for real estate firms, either.

There are dozens of true fiduciary real estate agents in Massachusetts. You should support their efforts and recommend a *True Loyal Agent*™ to your homebuying and homeselling clients.

Warn your real estate clients about Massachusetts *dual agency* or *designated agency* and refer them to MABA, The Massachusetts Association of Buyer Agents, 800-935-6222 or www.massbuyeragents.org, to find a dedicated *True Loyal Agent*™.

About the Author

Tom Wemett is a nationally known author, instructor, and homebuyer-representation specialist.

He started his own real estate brokerage and property management firm in the greater Rochester, New York, area in 1973.

In the late 1980s, Tom purchased a Help-U-Sell franchise that provided special marketing and sales programs for sellers.

The result wasn't what he expected.

The marketing drew in buyers, and Tom and his agents ended up spending more time helping buyers than helping sellers.

It was customary at the time for all real estate *licensees* to represent sellers legally but not buyers. Real estate *licensees* treated buyers as customers while they treated sellers as clients of the real estate company. The phenomenon started to change in the late 1980s with buyer representation becoming acceptable and desired by homebuyers.

Tom felt then that, when looking out for the best interest of a seller, it would be impossible also to look out for the best interest of a buyer of the same property.

This would create a conflict of interest as the seller wants the highest price and best terms for themselves and the buyer wants the lowest price and best terms for themselves.

For Tom the decision was clear and simple—represent one side exclusively and eliminate the conflict of interest of attempting to represent both a seller and a buyer on the same property in the same company.

In 1992, Tom became and continues today as an *exclusive buyer's agent* representing homebuyers only and never representing homesellers or taking listings.

He and his agents look out exclusively for the best interest of their homebuyer clients without compromise or conflict of interest.

Homebuyers want to buy the right home at the right price.

Tom's focus is to make sure that happens.

And Tom isn't alone. There are others out there who believe as Tom does that attempting to represent both a buyer and a seller on the same property within the same real estate company is impossible without compromising true representation of both.

However, the rest of the traditional real estate industry doesn't see it the same way and operates in a deeply ingrained sales culture that often leads to homebuyers being sold a home and short-changed without them even knowing.

As a result, Tom has dedicated his real estate career to supporting true fiduciary representation of both homebuyers and homesellers and was motivated to write this book specifically for homebuyers in Massachusetts.

Tom is the founder-broker-manager of Homebuyer Advisers LLC, an *exclusive buyer agency* currently operating in Florida and Massachusetts. Tom is a licensed real estate broker in Massachusetts, New York state, and Florida as well as a licensed real estate instructor in Florida.

He has earned several industry recognized designations including:

- Accredited Buyer Representative, ABR
- Accredited Buyer Representative Manager, ABRM
- Certified Exclusive Buyer Agent Master, CEBA-M
- Certified Buyer Representative, CBR
- Certified Buyer Agent, CBA
- Certified Residential Specialist, CRS
- Graduate REALTOR® Institute, GRI
- Certified Negotiation Expert, CNE
- Senior Real Estate Specialist, SRES
- Certified New Home Sales Professional, CSP
- Certified Homeowner Educator and Counselor, CHEC

Tom is an active member of the Massachusetts Association of Buyer Agents (MABA) and the National Association of Exclusive Buyer Agents (NAEBA).

He was a founding member of NAEBA and served as the NAEBA national president in 2003.

He serves on the board of directors of both MABA and NAEBA, as membership chair and chair of the agency task force for MABA, and as the director of membership for NAEBA.

Tom is a collaborating author for the third edition of the best selling book, *Not One Dollar More! How to Save $3,000 to $30,000 Buying Your Next Home*, by Joseph Eamon Cummins. Buy your copy online by going to: www.tomwemett.com/Not-One-Dollar-More

Tom can be reached at 978-633-9090 or by going to: www.tomwemett.com.

CPSIA information can be obtained
at www.ICGtesting.com
Printed in the USA
FSHW010814081118
53468FS